His
WORKMANSHIP

Reflections on living in Christ

Professor John Clark

Ark House Press
arkhousepress.com

Cataloguing in Publication Data:
Title: His Workmanship
ISBN: 9780645636697 (pbk)
Subjects: REL012120 [RELIGION / Christian Living / Spiritual Growth]; REL023000 [RELIGION / Christian Ministry / Discipleship]; REL108030 [RELIGION / Christian Living / Leadership & Mentoring]

Design by initiateagency.com

To my children and their partners; Katherine, Alexandra
and Rohan, Peter and Luella and to their children;

Olive, Genevieve, June, Mabel, Euan and Bernie

-*-*-*-*-*-*-*-*-*-*-*-*-*-*-*-*-*

Ephesians 2:10
For we are his workmanship, created in Christ
Jesus for good works, which God prepared
beforehand, that we should walk in them.

This book might never have been written without the support and encouragement of two people. The first is my friend and fellow believer, Dr John Goddard. His positive response to my initial sample of draft material was a vital impetus in actually proceeding with, and then completing, this project. I am also enormously grateful to John for giving so unstintingly of his extremely perceptive editorial skills in the appraisal of my completed drafts. John's professional experience in textual appraisal have been honed over a lifetime as a distinguished educator in English language and literature, and for the time and effort he has invested in my small project, I am more grateful than I can ever adequately say. The second is my wife Mary, whose love and support during our Christian walk together over these past fifty years and more, has sustained me with greater generosity than I have ever deserved. Without her constant presence and encouragement, I doubt that I would have embarked on this project at all. I cannot imagine having a more wonderful partner and friend in life. Above and beyond all this, I am truly thankful to God for His daily love, care and sustenance, and whose constant presence has allowed me to make sense of a world I would otherwise find both incomprehensible and intimidating.

CONTENTS

INTRODUCTION

W hy this book? A good question which every would-be author should be obliged to answer! The truth is, I didn't originally intend the material you see here to end up being published at all. It began because I was invited by my then church pastor to be an occasional guest preacher. By the grace of God I was already fairly used to standing in front of classes of adults as a tertiary education lecturer, so the process of public speaking, which I know fills some people with a degree of dread, was never a major issue. That said, as a layman I am acutely conscious of the limits to my largely self-taught knowledge of the Bible. At the same time, however, I have been both humbled and encouraged by positive reactions to my talks. People seem to have found them generally helpful in their Christian journey, and I give thanks to God for that because it is His doing alone. This is what has impelled me to revisit some of my preparation material from years past, and turn it into a collection of short reflections on some of the topics and Bible passages that I have been asked to talk about in church.

The choice of topics has in part been governed by the material available to me, but it is certainly not random. The first and last chapters explore who Jesus is, and how we should prepare for his return. Within these bookends, I have tried to use the light of Scripture to examine some of the basic challenges of our Christian walk which I think we should try to understand and integrate into our daily lives.

This book is therefore simply intended as a general and I trust Biblically faithful encouragement for my fellow everyday adult Christian believers or to genuine inquirers. I wanted it to be something folk could dip into as time and circumstance allowed, but not feel they would lose its thread if there were weeks, months, or even years between reads. Nothing in this book pretends, even for a moment, to be academic theology or doctrine. I am not a theologian! My primary hope is that readers will hear God speaking to them from His Word as I have tried to unpack and share what I believe it has to tell us on a number of topics which are fundamental to our Christian journey, and that as a consequence they will be encouraged to explore these topics more deeply. My prayer is that God will use this book to help bring each of us into a closer walk with Him so that our lives might reflect more closely the love and grace He has shown each of us in bringing us into a saving relationship with Jesus.

Soli Deo Gloria
John Clark
February 2023

Chapter 1
INTRODUCING JESUS

Some years back on a chilly 6th of January day, my wife and I found ourselves exploring the old part of the city of Seville in southern Spain where we came upon three locals dressed in colourful and rather elaborate robes that looked vaguely middle eastern. These splendidly attired gents seemed full of good cheer, were wishing everyone well, and handed out sweets to any passing children. Unbeknown to us, we had arrived in town on the Feast of the Epiphany, a traditional festival day which was first established in the eastern orthodox church. Today in Spain, it has become a highlight of the Christmas season and celebrates the arrival in Bethlehem of the Three Wise Men, or Magi, who were said to be the first gentiles to worship Jesus. This then, explains why some Spanish men go around the streets on January 6th all dressed up as they imagine the Magi might have looked over 2000 years ago.

To those of us who live in Australia, NZ, the UK, or North America, this might seem to be an unfamiliar, even slightly odd, Christmas tradition. Yet is it really any odder than some of the events that are a familiar part of our own Christmas festivities? In the city of Sydney, Carols in the Domain is a hugely popular public event that is held annually in a very large public park adjacent to the CBD. The program always contains an extraordinary mix of things, some of which, it must be said, have very tenuous connections indeed to the actual Christmas story. There are reindeer, Santa Claus, Disney characters, elves and TV celebrities, to name but some. And rather ironically, their appearances are all interleaved with renditions of wonderful carols like "Joy to the World", "Hark! the Herald Angels Sing" and "O Holy Night" which, despite the various accompanying distractions, continue to express the great central truths of the real Christmas message.

Popular ideas and understanding of the celebration of Christmas that are in any way genuinely Christian, mostly centre on the record of events about the birth of Jesus recorded in the gospels of Matthew and Luke. It is in these two books that we also learn about the stable, the shepherds, the angels and the wise men. On the other hand, the gospels of Mark and John don't give us any information at all about the birth and early life of Jesus. Instead, we first meet Jesus as He is just about to begin His ministry, and as He encounters John the Baptist. So it is no surprise that we really need all four gospels to give us the full picture of Jesus and who He is.

Now I know we all want our children and grandchildren to experience the joy and excitement of traditional Christmas festivities. But as believers, we also really want them to understand the central message of Christmas: the miracle of God being born in human form and bringing His long promised salvation to a fallen world. We want our children to grow up knowing that Christmas is about so much more than the shepherds, angels or wise men. Yes, these are certainly evidence of Jesus arriving in human form, but the real event is the arrival of Jesus

Himself. And much as we enjoy them, presents, christmas trees, Santa Claus, and many of our other various festive activities, are mostly traditions that have appeared in much later times.

As adults, one really helpful way to understand the Christmas story fully, is to begin by ensuring that we really know just who Jesus is. I want to try and do this here through the eyes of the apostle John, because His record provides us with an important and quite distinctive view of Jesus compared with the other three gospel accounts.

You might ask, just what it is that distinguishes John's gospel from the other three. Matthew, Mark, and Luke are known as the "synoptic" gospels, so called because they each provide, in varying degrees of detail, excellent summaries (synopses) of the life of Jesus. Scholars generally believe that Mark was the first gospel record, probably written early in the second half of the first century. Matthew and Luke come a little later, and very likely drew on Mark as well as other contemporary sources in compiling their own accounts of the life and work of Jesus.

John's account however, is quite different. So different in fact, that some critics have even doubted its authenticity. It contains no classic parables, no sermon on the mount, and not even the Lord's prayer. On the other hand it contains the earliest details of Jesus' Galilean ministry, and uniquely records notable miracles such as turning water into wine at the wedding feast in Cana, and then later, an account of the raising of Lazarus from the dead.

It seems almost certain that this gospel was written well after the other three, probably late in the 1st century. Scholars believe that John didn't try to duplicate the three earlier gospel records, but instead wanted to complement them, to fill in missing details, and provide some additional perspectives on Jesus himself. In this gospel we see Jesus in

His relationships with people, and we learn more about Jesus Himself, His deity, and about the person and work of the Holy Spirit.

Some of the earlier doubts held by scholars about the date of John's gospel have been dispelled by modern archaeology. One now largely discredited theory argued that the book had been written in the second century largely for Greek readers. Two relatively recent discoveries have helped prove this wrong. The first was the result of a Bedouin boy casually throwing a rock, as boys do, into a cave near the Dead Sea in 1947. The second began in even more unlikely circumstances, and was the result of sewer repairs in old Jerusalem in 2004. The Bedouin boy's rock led to the finding of the now world famous Dead Sea Scrolls in a saga that would have done Indiana Jones proud. These scrolls have proved to be an archaeological goldmine, providing historically important Hebrew texts, and valuable details of 1st century Jewish life which match well with the language and thinking of John's gospel. Then more than 50 years after this discovery, excavations for sewer repairs in old Jerusalem resulted in the rediscovery of the Pool of Siloam. Readers may recall that this was where *John 9:7* records that Jesus sent a blind man to have his sight restored. Having long been built over, for many years scholars had decided that it was a place which simply didn't exist! These discoveries have helped to date John's gospel and confirm its likely origins as late in the 1st century. This is all a great reminder never to doubt the reliability of God's Word.

When we compare the openings of the four gospels, the radically different perspective which John provides in his gospel record soon becomes obvious. Matthew starts by outlining the genealogy of Jesus back to Abraham and David, links this to the promise of a Messiah in *Malachi 3:1*, and then describes the birth of Jesus in detail. Mark avoids the nativity story completely, and gives a brief nod to the Old

Testament prophesies of a Messiah in **Malachi 3:1** and **Isaiah 40:3** before making a quick segue back to John the Baptist, and then introduces Jesus at the start of His ministry. Luke gives us the most complete history, including the births of both John the Baptist and Jesus. He acknowledges Jesus as the fulfilment of the OT prophesies in Isaiah and elsewhere, and not to be outdone by Matthew, Luke provides an extended genealogy right back to Adam! This radical difference in John's approach is evident right from the opening verses of his gospel in **John 1:1-3**

> *In the beginning was the Word, and the Word*
> *was with God, and the Word was God.*
> *He was in the beginning with God.*

Unlike the synoptic gospels, John begins by explaining the essential divinity of Jesus as part of the Godhead. Fully understanding the mind-bending concept of the Trinity is a significant challenge for all of us, but one so unquestionably important that we should work hard at trying to comprehend it. And that is exactly what these verses set out to do. It is no accident that the first words of both **Genesis 1** and **John 1** are the same, "In the beginning". Both refer to God the Father and God the Son; first in initiating the original creation described in Genesis, and then in introducing the new creation with the coming of Jesus. Part of the challenge here concerns the use of "the Word". It obviously refers to the Godhead, but in fact this probably isn't a great translation of the Hebrew, because "word" actually refers to God in action just as we see Him in the creation story. Every time God speaks something major happens.

In John's gospel record we meet Jesus immediately in verse 1 as the Lord of creation old and new. We meet Him as the one who has existed since before the beginning of time, and we meet Him as God, not just as the baby in our Christmas carols. We meet Him as God the Son who has actually come amongst us. Most importantly, we meet Jesus as God in human form who came to die and rise again to save us from our sins. Significantly, there isn't a shepherd, a wise man or a stable in sight! Instead, we get this breath-taking explanation of who Jesus really is, and the world-changing significance of His appearance.

In focusing on John's account, I am not wanting for one moment to dismiss the drama of Jesus' birth in Bethlehem which we all know and love. But at the same time, it is really important we also know and understand this part of the Christmas story in terms of salvation history, and recognise that what John presents to us is at the absolute core of the story. Unlike the three synoptic gospels, **John 1** starts the Christmas story not with the birth of Jesus as a baby, but with the theology that lies behind His appearance in human form, and then moves on into the events of history as John explains who Jesus really is and how His actual ministry begins.

Verses 2 and 3 immediately explain the deity of Jesus. John leaves us in absolutely no doubt of His eternal presence from the dawn of creation and of His integral role in the original creation process as **John 1:3** explains.

> *All things were made through Him, and without*
> *Him was not anything made that was made.*

Clearly Jesus was no bystander, He was God in action responsible for all of creation from day one. Nor does it stop there. **John 1:4&5** goes on to foreshadow that in His role as Creator He is also the source of the spiritual light available to us as believers during our earthly journey, dispelling sin and the darkness of unbelief, darkness which can never overcome that light.

In him was life, and the life was the light of men.
The light shines in the darkness, and the
darkness has not overcome it.

At this point the Gospel writer introduces us to John the Baptist, making it very clear that he is certainly not Jesus, that he is only there to prepare people for the appearance of Jesus. So we get a very clear explanation of how John the Baptist fits in as the herald for the coming of Jesus.

John must have cut quite a figure; described in the Bible as a fairly rustic looking hippy style character living out in the desert, dressed in camel hair, and living on basic bush food that he could find in the wilderness. Preaching, as he did, a message of repentance to the notoriously rebellious Israelites, he attracted quite a following. This was just as had been predicted in *Isaiah 40:3* about 700 years earlier, and then again in *Malachi 3:1* about 400 years later. *John 1:6-8* gives us a pretty good picture of the man and his ministry.

There was a man sent from God, whose name was John.
He came as a witness, to bear witness about the
light, that all might believe through him.
He was not the light, but came to bear
witness about the light.

Later in this chapter, we find John being interrogated by the Jewish authorities, curious about who this odd and eccentric character was, and what he was actually doing. There he again makes it very clear that he is just the messenger, certainly not the Messiah.

The problem was, that while the Jews desperately wanted the Messiah who was promised to them by the Old Testament prophets, they were, alas, looking in the wrong place. Under the oppressive rule of the Romans, the Jews of Jesus' time were looking for a political, not a spiritual, liberator. So even though he was careful to explain he wasn't the promised Messiah, they still wanted to know more about John's identity. Was He, perhaps, the prophet Elijah returned? And having ruled that out along with other possibilities, they were pretty frustrated, but they still wanted to know who he was, and what he was doing there. His response in *John 1:23* was:

> *I am the voice of one crying out in the*
> *wilderness, 'Make straight the way of the*
> *Lord,' as the prophet Isaiah said.*

This was a quote directly from *Isaiah 40:3* and the prophesy about John himself being the herald to the coming of Jesus. At this point the pharisees, who had come with the priests began to quiz John. They were a legalistic lot, mostly preoccupied with keeping the mosaic law in minutely irrelevant detail, and they were not happy with John's answer.

They wanted to know why he thought he had authority to baptise people if he wasn't the Messiah or even a prophet. It all begins to sound a bit like a classic union demarcation dispute. John's enigmatic answer probably left them even more puzzled. "Look" he said, "I'm just using water as a symbol of repentance, but there is someone here right now, someone you don't yet recognise, who will do far more". John was referring, whether he understood it at the time or not, to Jesus receiving the baptism of the Holy Spirit, which was the event that would empower Jesus to start His ministry. He then finishes in *John 1:25-28* by humbly comparing his own role to that of the lowest servant in a Jewish household, the one who undid the sandals and washed the feet of guests as they entered the house.

Finally, in **John 1:29-31** we meet Jesus Himself:

> *The next day he saw Jesus coming toward him,*
> *and said, "Behold, the Lamb of God, who*
> *takes away the sin of the world!*
> *This is he of whom I said, 'After me comes a man who*
> *ranks before me, because he was before me.'*
> *I myself did not know him, but for this purpose I came*
> *baptising with water, that he might be revealed to Israel."*

The idea of a lamb as a substitute sacrifice was a familiar one in Jewish culture. In **Genesis 22** God provided Abraham with a lamb in place of Isaac. In the events of **Exodus 12**, the Passover lamb was the substitute for the death of first born sons of Israelites to avoid a dreadful punishment intended only for their Egyptian overlords. In **Leviticus 4,** a lamb is prescribed as a personal sin offering, and in **Isaiah 53** the promised Messiah is described as being led like a lamb to the slaughter. The profound difference here is that Jesus is God's Lamb. This is God's final and all sufficient sacrificial provision across all human history for the whole of mankind. Nor does the image of the Lamb stop there. Again and again in the book of Revelation we find descriptions of Jesus as the Lamb in all His risen power, totally victorious over sin, death and Satan.

So, here we are about halfway through chapter 1 of John's gospel, and in just a single sentence, as we have seen in **John 1:29,** we have explained to us why Jesus was there; that God has given His Son to us as a sacrificial gift beyond all price, to bear the guilt of each and every last one of us.

Then in **John 1:30,31** John the Baptist explains that even though initially he didn't know who Jesus really was, he knew he'd been specifically sent as Jesus' herald, baptising people and preparing them for the public ministry of Jesus. But now he knows that Jesus is far greater than he is and in fact is John's own Creator and Redeemer coming from the beginning of time.

John's eyes had been opened to the true identity of Jesus. But just how had this happened? We know from the synoptic gospels that earlier on, Jesus Himself had come to John for baptism, and when He did, something remarkable had occurred as he explains in *John 1:32-34*

> *And John bore witness: "I saw the Spirit descend*
> *from heaven like a dove, and it remained on him.*
> *I myself did not know him, but he who sent me to baptise with*
> *water said to me, 'He on whom you see the Spirit descend*
> *and remain, this is he who baptises with the Holy Spirit.'*
> *And I have seen and have borne witness*
> *that this is the Son of God.*

In his act of water baptism, John had been privileged to witness something infinitely greater, Jesus receiving the baptism of the Holy Spirit. Suddenly he knew with God-given certainty, who Jesus really was, and that Jesus in turn would baptise people not with water, but with the Holy Spirit. That is why he could now say with absolute certainty "this is the Son Of God".

Baptism of the Spirit, as we have seen, marks the start of the earthly ministry of Jesus, and it fulfils the Messianic prophesies in *Isaiah 11:2, 42:1* and elsewhere, that "the spirit of the Lord will rest on Him". This is really important, so it is no surprise that all four gospels describe it. But in recording this momentous event, only John makes the important point in verse 32 that the Spirit remained upon Jesus, which is why further on in *John 3:34* John the Baptist explains that Jesus has the Holy

Spirit without limit. In turn, it is Jesus who has then promised every believer the baptism and indwelling presence of the Holy Spirit, as He explains in far more detail in *John 16*.

I think the way these events are recorded in John's gospel provide a really valuable and quite deliberately alternative take on the traditional Christmas story. As I observed earlier, there are no shepherds, no wise men, no angels, no cattle, none of the usual Christmas trappings. Yet in just a few verses of this opening chapter we get a remarkable picture of Jesus as the Lord of creation, Jesus as part of the Godhead, and Jesus as the sacrificial Lamb by whose death and resurrection we are offered reconciliation with God in all His holiness, and so eternal life.

Again, I must stress that in exploring this alternative perspective on the Christmas story as provided by John, I am not for a moment wanting to dismiss the value and the delight we get from celebrating the traditional nativity story; the wonder of the appearance of God humbly entering the world in human form as a newborn baby. It is a unique and quite extraordinary story, and one always worthy of celebration. But when all is said and done, is this remarkable event what are we really celebrating? In one sense, I don't think so. We celebrate the birth of Jesus, not because he came in the form of a cute little baby housed, for lack of an alternative, in an animal feed trough. No, we celebrate the miraculous arrival of God amongst us in human form, coming here so that He could take away the sins of the world. We celebrate God's amazing gift of Jesus as the One who can rescue us from condemnation for all our shortcomings, the One who, despite all our human imperfection, can reconcile us with our perfect and holy God. We celebrate a gift of grace to us which is generous beyond all human comprehension. This is the core of what we really celebrate; certainly not the arrival of three middle eastern gents wearing fancy apparel and carrying exotic presents. Because if that was all there was to Christmas, frankly it would just be the tragic story of a failed would-be prophet, largely forgotten, whose life ended in a sad and quite shameful death.

Yet as we know, that is not how Jesus' life unfolded. As Christians, this alternative version of the Christmas story should help focus our attention on one of the key reasons for celebrating His coming. As we have seen, **John 1** records Jesus receiving the baptism of the Spirit at the start of His ministry. He in turn offers this gift to every single believer as an integral part of accepting Jesus as their Lord and Saviour. We don't accept Jesus as our Saviour out of intellectual conviction, it is the work of the Holy Spirit within us that brings us to faith, and then it is His ongoing presence in our lives that sustains our faith. We just wouldn't survive on our Christian journey if we were on our own. I asked Jesus to be my Lord and Saviour more years ago than I care to count, and like most Christians, my journey since has had its ups and downs. But as I write these words today, I am certain of what God has done for me in Christ as my redeemer only because the Holy Spirit has sustained my faith day by day. It has been a spiritual journey that has only been possible because I have always travelled in His care. It is certainly none of my doing.

So as we reflect on this passage, we should thank God every day for His faithfulness in keeping His promises made through the prophets of old to send Jesus as our Saviour. It is also a gentle reminder, at Christmas time especially, not to be overly distracted by images and stories of a baby born in rather agricultural circumstances. But when we do start there, we need to be certain that we see the whole picture, and ensure we thank God, that just as Jesus came to us born in normal human form, in manhood he received the empowering baptism of the Spirit at the start of His earthly ministry. We should thank God as believers, both that He sent Jesus to die and rise victorious as our Redeemer, and that He left His gift of the baptism and the presence of the Holy Spirit within us to make our journey of faith through this fallen world to eternity possible.

Chapter 2
GRACE

C hris (short for Christian) was a really keen churchgoer. Never missed a Sunday, served for years on his Parish Council, ran a Bible study group, helped with the men's ministry, and worked on the church cleaning team. Then one day, deep in thought and not paying much attention to the traffic, he stepped onto the road. There was a screech of brakes and suddenly he found himself in a large empty room.

Chris gathered his wits and quite quickly realised that he was now dead. The Mack truck had done a really thorough job on him. Then, before he had time for any further thought, a guy in a smart rather well cut suit, and looking a bit like a TV game show host, appeared from nowhere. "Hi Chris," he said cheerily. "Welcome! I'm St Peter".

Chris was completely flabbergasted and stammered a reply, "Uh, hello," adding "I, err, I thought you would be really old, I thought you'd have a long white beard and a harp, and be dressed in a flowing white robe. I thought I'd hear wonderful choral music and see bright lights and angels everywhere".

"Oh that's a very old-fashioned idea of life up here", said St Peter. "Things are a bit different nowadays. You see, Himself has had the management consultants in, and you are actually in our new off-shore processing facility. These days we use key performance indicators to assess applicants like you. To make it into heaven, you need 100 points which, if you'll pardon the pun, is dead easy. You just tell me all the good things you've done, and I'll tell you what they're worth on your KPI score".

"OK!" said Chris, who by now was starting to feel pretty relaxed. "Well for starters, I was married for over 30 years and was never ever unfaithful to my dear wife."

"Great" said St. Peter, "three points!"

"Only three points?" said Chris, "Gosh, well........ OK, I attended church every Sunday, I gave generously and supported all of our ministries."

"I should hope so!" observed St. Peter, "two points."

"Just two points? Oh boy! Well, um, how about this. I worked on the church cleaning roster and cooked hundreds of meals for the youth group on Sunday nights."

"Hmmm, very commendable," remarked St. Peter. "Two more points."

"Only two points!!" gulped Chris, by now becoming somewhat alarmed.

"Anything else useful on your CV?" inquired St Peter

"Well yes, in fact there is. For years I ran a Bible study group for the spiritually dysfunctional."

"I'm sure you were very well suited to that," said St Peter drily. "At a pinch, perhaps another three points"

By now Chris had become very silent; his initial confidence had completely evaporated, and panic was setting in. Then he brightened up. "Hang on," he said, feverishly searching his wallet. "I've got my Inter-Church Council Heavenly Points Gold Card right here!"

St Peter gave it a rather uninterested glance.

"But look at the signature!" said Chris

St Peter held it up and said "Hmm......can't quite make out the name, looks like an archbishop of some sort, not that it really matters. But I will grant you it is a charming piece of ecclesiastical memorabilia," and he promptly tossed it into a waste bin which had very conveniently just materialised." So, Chris,........is that it?"

"Errrrr .....yes" said Chris. "But look at all this good stuff I've done, and all I've made is a mere 10 points......10 miserable points!" and with that he collapsed on the floor sobbing. "My case is hopeless. The only way I'll get into heaven is by the grace of God!"

"Yes, Yes!" said a delighted St Peter "I told you it was dead easy, grace **is** the only way anyone can ever get 100 points. Please do come right on in!"

This story is of course just a ridiculous figment of my probably over-developed human imagination, just a 21st century man speculating about what we might face entering heaven after leaving this present life. But even though this story is completely fanciful, it illustrates an important point. We can never, ever, be saved by our own works, no matter how worthwhile or virtuous they might seem. It is only by God's grace in sending Jesus to bear the punishment for all our sins person-ally, all our mistakes and all our human shortcomings, that we can be redeemed and made worthy to enter the presence of God in all His holiness. Paul and the other new testament writers are at great pains to make sure we understand that under no circumstances can we ever earn our own salvation.

God's grace is a central theme of chapter 2 in Paul's letter to the church at Ephesus, and if we want to make proper sense of what Paul means in this letter about the riches of God's grace, we first need to understand what he's written in chapter 1. This is a detailed exposition of all that God has done for His creation. It is Paul at his most brilliant as he explains the perfection and the completeness of God's plan of salvation in Christ. This is the message of *John 3:16*, but now fully unpacked in all its amazing detail. Here Paul lays out the past, present, and future of God's great plan of salvation; and all of it seen from God's point of view. As we read the opening chapter of this letter, we can sense Paul's real joy as he describes the incredible blessings we have as believers, and will continue to receive in Christ, culminating in His return when all of creation becomes subject to Jesus Himself. *Ephesians 1:7-10* provides an excellent summary.

> *In him we have redemption through his blood,*
> *the forgiveness of our trespasses, according to the*
> *riches of his grace, which he lavished upon us, in all*
> *wisdom and insight making known to us the mystery*
> *of his will, according to his purpose, which he set forth*
> *in Christ as a plan for the fullness of time, to unite all*
> *things in him, things in heaven and things on earth.*

In other words, God loved us so much that He sent His son Jesus to take the punishment for all our sins, and He did this in His grand plan to rescue us from ourselves, and ultimately and finally to unite all creation in Christ.

Having explained salvation from God's point of view, Paul then goes on in *Ephesians 2* to look at salvation from the viewpoint of the individual Christian starting, very uncomfortably for us, with what we were before God laid His hand on us. He explains what God has done in saving us, and what we are now to be as a consequence of experiencing such great salvation. This is about the past, present and future of every Christian, up close and very personal.

As we come to **Ephesians 2:1-3,** there is no gentle lead-in. Paul goes straight for the jugular as he suddenly puts us under the microscope with just two words: *"And you...."*

> *And you were dead in the trespasses and sins in*
> *which you once walked, following the course of this world,*
> *following the prince of the power of the air, the spirit that*
> *is now at work in the sons of disobedience among whom*
> *we all once lived in the passions of our flesh, carrying*
> *out the desires of the body and the mind, and were by*
> *nature children of wrath, like the rest of mankind.*

Now when Paul says *"dead"*, he really does mean dead. Many liberal thinkers have rather objected to this idea. They would say there is a lot of evidence that over the course of history, mankind has been improving. Compared to the past, they would claim, we care more about social equity and welfare, we give more generously to the relief of human need, and many more people volunteer to work on humanitarian aid projects. Whether this is, or is not, really true depends at least in part on how philanthropy is measured. But that of course is only part of the picture. Look at the daily violence and death toll in regions like the Middle East and Africa, look at the gun violence in the USA, look at the millions of people living in camps as displaced refugees, look at the aggressive erosion of moral values in our own society and others like it, full of corruption, deception, and infidelity. Alas, it doesn't paint a pretty picture. We cannot escape the fact that we live in a fallen world that is very far from perfect. Since the fall itself this has always been true. Since then, it has never been perfect, and it never will be until Jesus returns. This is not just about the rest of society, it starts with us. Who of us would really like all of our darkest secrets made public? Make no mistake, whether we like it or not, mankind is innately evil, and since the fall always has been. And it follows that if we are spiritually dead, as verse 2 reminds us, then consciously or not we are inevitably followers of Satan. *"All have sinned and fall short of the glory of God,"* Paul wrote in **Romans 3:23**. "All" here means you and it means me just as much as it means the worst terrorist, murderer or sex offender.

But the greatest tragedy of all is that for unbelievers it means their relationship with God is inherently dead, and that there is nothing they themselves can do which will ever change that. And worse, in this dead and sinful state every unbeliever, no matter how respectable they might seem to be, will stand condemned under God's judgement. I know it isn't fashionable nowadays to preach "turn or burn" style sermons with lurid accounts of human depravity and the excruciating punishments of hell. I am thinking here, for example, of the sort of thing you can find in James Joyce's novel *"A Portrait of the Artist as a Young Man"*.

"Hell is a strait and dark and foul-smelling prison, an abode of demons and lost souls, filled with fire and smoke.......The horror of this strait and dark prison is increased by its awful stench. All the filth of the world, we are told, shall run there as to a vast reeking sewer..."

Descriptions of hell like this, and worse, are quite hair-raising for a modern reader living in an age when we get uncomfortable even talking quite generally about the judgement of God. But the Bible is inescapably clear that without experiencing God's redeeming grace we are, and will remain, spiritually dead, utterly condemned no matter how respectable a life we might live. In fact, one of the real dangers of living, as some of us do, in nice, peaceful and respectable parts of the planet, is to risk deluding ourselves that as human beings we really aren't too bad compared to many people elsewhere. But no matter who we are, no matter how respectable we might appear to be, the reality is that without God we are utterly lost, and God alone can take us from death to spiritual life. Only by God's grace can we avoid His condemnation and, in whatever form it takes, eternal separation from Him.

At this point you might well be asking why I have gone on at such length about sin and judgement when it all seems just so depressing. It's true, it is far from being a cheery subject. However, I've hammered this point for a very good reason which is simply this: you and I will never ever fully, personally, and intimately understand the immense riches of God's grace to us, and the completely undeserved love He has lavished on us, until we first fully confront what we are really like as individuals without Him. We need to recognise and admit our comprehensively sinful nature. If we cling to the delusion that really, we aren't as bad as many of our fellow human beings, and if we aren't prepared to confront what it really means to recognise that on our own we are totally, helplessly lost, and spiritually dead, then we will never fully understand the depth of God's grace in sending Jesus to take all our sin upon Himself. That is the whole point of Paul's analysis of you and me, and indeed of all mankind. He brings us to the foot of the Cross with absolutely no merit of our own to offer God. This is the blunt truth of the state of the human condition without God's forgiveness, and ultimately it is the only reality that actually matters.

Then, just as abruptly as he has put us under the microscope at the start of Chapter 2, Paul contrasts our hopeless condition with the salvation God offers us, again using two dramatic and transforming words in *Ephesians 2:4-7* "*But God*". These two simple words this time take us from a picture of complete despair to the threshold of the wonder, the miracle, the pure joy and the grace of the Gospel. These two words preface Paul's description of the great news of God's amazing gift of full and permanent rescue from spiritual death that He offers us as His creation: ***"But God…"***.

> ***But God, being rich in mercy, because of the great love with which he loved us, even when we were dead in our trespasses, made us alive together with Christ - by grace you have been saved - and raised us up with Him and seated us with Him in the heavenly places in Christ Jesus, so that in the coming ages He might show the immeasurable riches of His grace in kindness toward us in Christ Jesus.***

God in His infinite goodness never ever intended to abandon us. We are His creation, we are made in His image, and completely undeserving as we are God in His grace and mercy so loved us, as ***John 3:16*** tells us, so loved us unconditionally, that He gave us Jesus who by His death and resurrection has paid the price of our sin in full. By His sacrifice, if we truly believe what He has done, we are reconciled to God in all His holiness, so that despite our sins and our many failures we will not fall under His judgement. As Martin Luther discovered some five hundred years ago as he studied Paul's letter to the Romans, we are justified in God's sight by faith alone in the death and resurrection of Jesus. This is the unique miracle of God's grace at work. In His great love He planned from the dawn of time to save us from our own wickedness when we were spiritually dead, when in our human frailty we were absolutely unable to help ourselves, and when He could have simply abandoned us as a hopeless cause. But in the wonder of His grace, undeserving as we are, by the indwelling power of the Holy Spirit He will reach out and save us if we will only believe what Jesus has done for us.

God's grace doesn't end there. When we are "raised up with Christ", we cease just to be part of the fallen sinful world, we have a completely new life. We are now united with Jesus, we are part of His Kingdom, we share in His victory on the cross over sin and death, we now see life through His eyes, we know and acknowledge that He is the Lord of all creation. And we are now on our journey with Jesus to an eternity in heaven where we will live forever in the light of God's glory. And even though right now we still have to live with all the imperfections of this fallen world, by the power of God continuing to work in us, if our faith is real, our lives will reflect this greater transcendent experience and the expectations it brings that can come only from being "raised with Christ". Our transformed life is the fruit of the Gospel. Fragile and imperfect we may still be, but it is the external and visible evidence of God's redeeming grace at work within us

Ever the realist, Paul explains what this should actually mean here and now in *Colossians 3:1,2:*

> *If then you have been raised with Christ, seek the things that are above, where Christ is, seated at the right hand of God. Set your minds on things that are above, not on things that are on earth.*

We all need to ask ourselves, is this our experience as a follower of Jesus? Has it changed our lives completely and permanently? If our faith is real, if we have confessed Jesus as our lord and saviour, He will have taken us from helpless spiritual death to a transformed life that is already a taste of heaven to come, and we will know it. So why did God do all this for his disobedient creation? He did it , as Paul explained in *Ephesians 1* to show us, undeserving as we are, the boundless richness of His grace and His measureless love for us. More than that, He did it to demonstrate the majesty and the glory of who He is. I don't think we will ever really get our heads around the enormity of what God has done for us until we join Jesus in heaven. Right now we can only marvel in our limited human way at the boundless grace and love of the Lord we serve.

Paul famously reminds us in *Ephesians 2:8,9* that it is God's grace alone that has saved us.

> *For by grace you have been saved through faith.*
> *And this is not your own doing; it is the gift of God,*
> *not a result of works, so that no one may boast.*

Verses 8 & 9, are amongst some of the best known in the New Testament. God in His infinite grace sent His Son to save us, and in His infinite grace has given us the faith we need to confess Jesus our Lord and Saviour. None of this is our doing, every last bit is God's grace alone at work in us. If you want some sobering proof of this, take a look at *Matthew 25:44* where Jesus describes the last judgement. Those who were truly saved couldn't even remember the good deeds they had done. Those doomed to hell did all the boasting about their actions in life. As I have laboured at length to explain here, the Bible tells us clearly and unequivocally that we are saved by God's grace and by that grace alone.

I spent my childhood living in my grandparents' house, and my grandmother was a godly Christian woman. She made very sure that from an early age I knew what Jesus had done for me, and so I entered my teens assuming that I understood and believed this. But when I was 16 and joined a confirmation class, mostly I might add, because a schoolmate was there as well, I heard with fresh ears what God had done for me in sending Jesus to die for my sin, and as I walked home one night from that class more than half a century ago, God in His grace reached out to me, and for the first time through the power of the Holy Spirit I truly understood what it meant to call Jesus my Lord and Saviour. This was all God's doing and absolutely none of mine. And through the miracle of His ongoing grace, in His strength alone, despite all my human frailty I have remained united and raised with Christ just as scripture has promised.

A key part of God's ongoing work of grace in our lives as believers is to sustain our faith by the indwelling of the Holy Spirit. This is just as well, because we certainly could not do it in our own strength. This is why, against all human odds and despite all the doubts, fears and human failures we experience as part of everyday life, God by the indwelling power of the Holy Spirit sustains us on our heavenward journey. This is why Paul could write so confidently in **Romans 8:38&39:**

> *For I am sure that neither death nor life,*
> *nor angels nor rulers, nor things present nor things*
> *to come, nor powers, nor height nor depth, nor*
> *anything else in all creation, will be able to separate*
> *us from the love of God in Christ Jesus our Lord.*

Paul's great confidence in these words of assurance comes from experiencing the ongoing work of God's grace in his own very eventful life, from no longer living as a serial persecutor of Christians, but instead becoming an ambassador for Jesus. What a spectacular turnaround as he spread the gospel across the Mediterranean world, as he founded churches and encouraged believers, knowing every day just what it was like to be raised with Christ. Do you and I always feel that same confidence? Have you had moments when your faith has really been shaken? I know I have, and that is the time when we need to claim the grace which God promises will always be there in these verses from Romans, and always available, when in our need we turn to Him.

As a long time believer, by God's grace let me also add a word of warning. As I've experienced the ups and downs of life, made my full share of horrible mistakes as I have tried to serve God in various ways, I confess I have sometimes been tempted to feel that spiritually I've been earning my keep a bit, rather like the guy in our opening story. Cleaning the church, serving on parish council, being a youth leader, contributing to missionary work etc. etc. But these verses from *Ephesians 2* always shout "No!" at me ."This is not your own doing! Your faith isn't the result of anything you did....never!" The18[th] Century hymn writer Augustus Toplady captured the core truth of this as well as anyone in the hymn "Rock of Ages", when he wrote *"nothing in my hand I bring, simply to the Cross I cling"*. I know of no better acknowledgement that our relationship with God is only possible by our complete reliance on His grace and mercy.

So.... if you and I are tempted to feel even a little bit good about the way we serve the work of the Gospel, please don't! Read and re-read these verses, and just thank God every day that part of His work of grace in each of us is that however imperfectly we do it, He allows us the privilege of humbly serving Him, but doing so in His strength alone.

It would be easy to conclude from all I have said, that maybe Christian service is a bit irrelevant, or worse, might actually risk making us feel as if our works are important. But not so: if we really understand that we should serve the Lord as He has planned for each of us, this should surely help us keep our service in a proper spiritual perspective. I think that *Ephesians 2:10* explains how this works very simply and very clearly. The verse is one of my favourites, and it leaps out at me every time I read it.

*For we are his workmanship, created in Christ
Jesus for good works, which God prepared
beforehand, that we should walk in them.*

This verse is yet another great reminder that we are no longer the subjects of Satan. Instead, that we have been raised with Christ, that we are God's workmanship, created in Christ for good works. Or as Paul puts it in *2Corinthians 5:17 :*

If anyone is in Christ He is a new creation.

And the part of **Ephesians 2:10** which I especially like is Paul's reminder that God has always had a plan for each one of us. This is another aspect of the grace He gives us when we are raised with Christ. There is not a Christian on the planet, be they nine or ninety nine, for whom God does not have Gospel related work to do. We should be thankful every day that God doesn't just leave us here to muddle about on our own. Praise God that salvation isn't an isolated, one off event after which God says "Now off you go, and good luck!"

When we are raised with Christ, and are His workmanship, when we are members of His Kingdom, He is with us on every step of our spiritual journey through the presence and the power of the Holy Spirit within us until we join Him in heaven. This is part of God's continuing work of grace in our lives; our daily challenge is to open our hearts to Him, to let Him exercise that grace within us, and so to let Him lead and empower us in everything we do. In writing to the church in Ephesus **(Ephesians 2:19)** Paul also reminds his readers of their place in God's family, a reminder that applies just as much to us today in our earthly journey.

So then you are no longer strangers and aliens,
but you are fellow citizens with the saints
and members of the household of God.

When I retired, I got heartily sick of people asking me how I was filling in my time. Give me a break! God has given me more exciting opportunities to serve Him in a variety of gospel-related ministries than I could have ever expected, and it just goes on happening. It has been a joy and a privilege for me to try and serve the Lord both when I was working, and now in retirement, and I do hope this is true for you too. If you and I, no matter how old or young we may be, are really raised with Christ, and really understand what it means to be God's workmanship, then the proof of that will show in what we do with our time. I know that in our day to day Christian lives it is all too easy to feel a bit left out, maybe even a bit helpless, a bit uncertain as to how we fit in, or even a bit useless. But friends, take heart from verse 10; as I explained earlier we need to let God exercise His grace in us by believing and claiming His promised plan for each of us. And if my own experience is any guide, He expects us to seek out His will actively, and not just sit around passively expecting opportunities for Christian service simply to fall in our laps. God's ongoing work of grace in our lives is always there for the asking, but we have a responsibility to seek His will actively . We know from **Ephesians 2:10** that He has promised that He has a plan for everyone, and therefore He expects that we will prayerfully and responsibly work to learn what that plan might be, and then act upon it. This is one practical way to give glory to God as we experience His ongoing work of grace in our everyday lives.

One final word. If as you have read this chapter, you feel unsure whether you have experienced God's saving grace at work in your life, if you are not sure that you can confidently call Jesus your Lord and Saviour, please talk to a Christian friend or pastor and ask Jesus to be your redeemer. It is the single most important decision you will ever make.

Chapter 3
FAITH

R adio talk show hosts often give listeners the impression that they think they know everything. Few of them ever seem at all shy about offering their opinions on everything under the sun to their sometimes less than critical audience. These guys are always on the lookout for stories that are in one way or another sensational and offer a chance for making controversial claims of various kinds. They are not called "Shock Jocks" for nothing. So it will come as no surprise that, so the story goes, one of them started keeping tabs on the Covid virus when it first appeared, thinking it might provide some useful program material, if of course it actually turned out to be real. As we all now know, the virus quickly spread, became a pandemic, and everyone was asked to wear a mask.

Our talk show host just ignored this directive, told his listeners the seriousness of the virus was very likely exaggerated and that, anyway, this mask stuff was a violation of civil liberties, adding that it was still possible the whole thing was just a hoax. More and more people got sick, the death toll started to rise, and he finally had to admit it wasn't a hoax but still assured everyone he had faith that God would protect him. Vaccines appeared offering high levels of protection from the virus, which meant if you did catch it and were vaccinated, you were far less likely to experience severe illness. Our radio man was offered a choice of jabs but he turned them all down, still saying he believed God would protect him. He didn't want the government interfering in his life, much less turning him into a guinea-pig for the products of big pharmaceutical companies.

Then came the lockdowns, mostly in places where the death toll was really high and the virus was spreading rapidly. People were given a government directive to stay home, and not to entertain any visitors. Everyone just hated it. Some lost their jobs, businesses collapsed, home schooling became a nightmare for parents, and normal social life all but ground to a halt. People generally started getting a bit stir crazy! Our talk show host was increasingly outraged at this escalating assault on civil liberty, so eventually he broke curfew, left home and joined a big and largely unmasked, protest group in the city. A few days later, he started to feel unwell, tested positive for Covid and then got really sick. He ended up in his local hospital ICU where he didn't respond well to treatment, soon needed oxygen, and eventually was put on a ventilator. Despite the best efforts of the medical staff, he finally died. As a believer, he went to heaven, and immediately started complaining to God. " I don't understand!" he said. " Why didn't you protect me? Why did I die of Covid ? I had faith in You! I prayed that you would look after me, but you just let me die!"

God looked at him and said "You had faith? What kind of faith? I answered all your prayers several times over. I sent masks which you dismissed, then lock-downs to stop infection spreading which you disobeyed, I stopped people socialising, but you just laughed off all these precautions. I provided you with a choice of vaccines, any of which would certainly have saved your life, and you refused them. Despite your claim to have faith, you rejected them all. What more did you possibly expect?"

This obviously hypothetical little story has some close parallels to real life in the way some people have reacted to the Covid pandemic. Very importantly, it also illustrates some of the rather strange ideas they have about faith and how it works. The great American man of letters H.L. Mencken once cynically observed that *"faith may be defined as "an illogical belief in the occurrence of the improbable"* and in human terms, he may just have been nearer to the truth than he intended. Voltaire got a little closer when he said that *"faith consists in believing when it is beyond the power of reason to believe. It is not enough for a thing to be possible for it to be believed."*

So what went wrong for the radio host in our cautionary tale? It is pretty simple really. He just didn't understand the real nature of faith. We can see that in his actions. It didn't help that he was used to people accepting his rather self-centred opinions on almost everything. He thought faith was just believing that the things he wanted really would happen. Because he hardly believed the virus was life threatening, he thought that he was nearly invulnerable, and he would never get sick, let alone become seriously ill. But truth to tell, he had the whole idea of faith upside down. Faith doesn't start with us, it always starts with God. It is God who made us, and God who ultimately controls His creation. God never promises we'll always just get what we want if we have enough faith. Having faith is first and foremost about trusting and accepting what He wants for each of us. Because God made us, He always knows far better than we do what is best for us.

Faith is a really important topic in the Bible. The word appears there between about 300 and 500 times, depending on the translation. It is a major topic in the letter to the Hebrews which examines this whole question of faith in some detail, and which is why it is going to be our focus here. **Hebrews** is an unusual letter, in some ways even a bit mysterious. It doesn't have quite the same personal feel we find in letters written to specific churches or people as for example in **Philippians**, **Galatians** or **1&2Timothy**. Nor are we entirely sure who wrote it, or even exactly when in the first century it was written. What we do know is that it sets out a really comprehensive defence of the gospel as the fulfilment of the revealing of the Kingdom of God through the coming of Jesus. We also know that it is addressed specifically to a Jewish audience in the context of their history and unique understanding of God's dealing with them as His people. It is obvious the writer is quite familiar with this history, and has made effective use of it to explain just how God has dealt first with Israel, and then with the gentile world now that Jesus has come as the long promised final revelation of God's Kingdom. It is intended to encourage persecuted Jewish Christians in the early church to persevere in their newfound faith in Jesus as the final fulfilment of the Old Testament promises of a Messiah, and not to be tempted to revert to their former faith based on the now supplanted Mosaic Law.

As we try to get a better understanding of faith, let me zero in on **Hebrews 11**. Again, depending on the translation, **"faith"** gets used over 30 times in Hebrews, and more than 20 of these occurrences are found in **Hebrews 11** alone. No wonder this chapter is sometimes called "God's Hall of Faith"!

The whole object of **Hebrews 11** is to encourage us to live by faith; to take heart from the lives of God's servants of old, people who often had nothing but His promises to hang on to. These people sometimes had absolutely no evidence God's promises would come to anything, yet they lived out their lives as if these same promises had already been made good. This is what true faith is all about, and **Hebrews 11** is packed with great examples of faith, people believing absolutely in God's promises, not just hoping for personal pipe-dreams to come good.

We don't have the space here to explore all the examples found in this chapter, but let's at least look at a few, and I trust they will encourage readers to explore the remainder. **Hebrews 11:1** begins with an excellent working definition:

> **Now faith is the assurance of things hoped**
> **for, the conviction of things not seen.**

In other words, faith is what gives us the conviction that God will do exactly what He has promised. In the Bible, He has made promises of salvation that begin way back in the Old Testament. Here in the 21st century we know that He has now fulfilled these promises by sending Jesus to offer us redemption and eternal life through His death and resurrection. This we now know was the pivot point in human history.

Faith has sometimes been described as the quality which, in a spiritual sense, allows us to "see" God, and so to trust completely that He is who He says He is, and to believe absolutely that He will do what He says He will do. Obviously this isn't an "intellectual" proof of His existence and His actions, and God has never said that we should expect such a proof for His claims. What we read instead in **Hebrews 11** is a series of real life examples of faith as it has actually worked in the lives of real people.

These then, were people who "saw" God through their faith, and what we read here is designed to encourage us to do the same. This is why **Hebrews 12** begins by saying:

> *Therefore, since we are surrounded by so great a*
> *cloud of witnesses, let us also lay aside every weight,*
> *and sin which clings so closely, and let us run with*
> *endurance the race that is set before us.*

We also need to understand that the examples of faith set out **Hebrews 11** aren't just a random collection of historical anecdotes. Far from it. These examples carefully trace the course of salvation history from God's first revelation of Himself in creation, right through to Jesus as the fulfilment of that revelation. This is why **Hebrews 11:3** goes right back to the very beginning of everything:

> *By faith we understand that the universe was*
> *created by the word of God, so that what is seen*
> *was not made out of things that are visible.*

Faith begins when we acknowledge that it was God who created the universe and our world, that it was God who established and sustains the space-time relationships which enable it to continue operating, that it was God who created the life which inhabits it. And don't forget this: that before God created, there was nothing else there.

All this is fundamental to faith. Do we seriously think that our post-modern, silicon chip, information-obsessed, world is really the result of some arbitrary cosmic hiccup which accidentally set in motion events that then by happenstance led to our 21st century society? If we do, then we have no hope of exercising real faith in any of God's claims.

But if we do believe He is the creator of an ordered universe where none existed before, then it follows we should also have faith that He retains ultimate control over its operation, its future, and very importantly, our place in it.

Hebrews 11:4 brings us to the first of the key characters in the "Hall of Faith" I mentioned earlier: Abel, who unhappily also has the dubious distinction of being the first ever recorded homicide victim.

Abel was murdered by his brother Cain in a fit of jealous rage, and he is an example of faith because God saw him as a "righteous" man. We can only speculate as to exactly what it was that pleased God about his life more than Cain's. We are only told that he lived by his faith, and that even in death his life and witness still spoke, ironically the very thing Cain wanted to silence.

Hebrews 11:5 then introduces one of the Bible's rather unusual figures, Enoch. He is also incidentally famous as the father of the man who lived for so long that every superannuation fund manager should fear him - Methuselah! We know little about Enoch's life, yet his commendation is complete, because *Genesis 5:24* simply says:

Enoch walked with God, and he was not, for God took him.

Faith put Enoch into a special relationship in which we are told that he pleased God. At the end of his long life the Bible records that God took him from the earth and we are also told that he didn't experience death in any conventional sense. *Hebrews 11:6* then goes on to remind us that we cannot please God without faith, and that we cannot know God unless we first believe He exists. The verse ends with an assurance that He will reward everyone who genuinely seeks to know Him.

Some people just don't get it that we can't please God by our good works. We must start and end with a total reliance on Him, and with what He has done for us in Christ. Only in our redeemed relationship can we look forward in faith to God watching over us, guiding us, and ultimately bringing us into His eternal Kingdom.

Hebrews 11:7 brings us to Noah, someone we know a lot more about than either Enoch or Abel. Noah literally laid his faith on the line for everyone to see. He is a great practical example of a man publicly living out his faith, whereas the radio shock-jock clearly didn't, as I explained at the start of the chapter.

Noah must have had quite a time of it with his neighbours. Can you imagine having some religious nutter living in your street setting out to build a three decker boat about the size of a modern coastal freighter in his back yard? And not only that, doing it miles from the sea! He was lucky he didn't live in a modern local government area or he would probably still be waiting for planning permission! Can you picture the derision of his neighbours as this seemingly misguided project just went on and on? But throughout this whole DIY saga Noah's faith in God's directions to make preparations to survive a massive flood was undeterred, and as the Bible records, he was saved along with his whole family. His backyard boat had been successfully built to withstand an extreme weather event that would likely have made a modern tropical cyclone look like a passing shower. And if all that wasn't enough, you really have to admire the man's courage for letting himself be locked up with his relatives for months on end in a floating zoo!

Noah's faith was also rewarded in a far greater way. He had God's blessing as he re-established family life, and as the flood subsided God made good His promise to preserve him and his future generations. Noah is a great example of faith rewarded by God exercising his grace both immediately and in the long term.

Hebrews 11:8 brings us to Abraham. Here is a man we know even more about, a man who demonstrated his faith by taking God at His word. You can read his whole amazing story starting in *Genesis 12*. He left the comfort and security of his father's household in the ancient city of Ur, which was located in the general region around northern Syria, southern Turkey and northern Iraq. Nobody today is entirely sure of the exact spot. He set out on a new life, uncertain just where he would end up, or what dangers and hardships he would encounter. Most importantly, in embarking on this journey into the unknown, Abraham was simply being faithful to God's direction. As Abraham and his wife got older they had no children of their own, yet God made them the seemingly improbable promise of a family which would eventually become a whole nation. It was seemingly improbable because it flew in the face of normal biological possibility. Yet Abraham and his wife Sarah had faith in this extraordinary promise, and true to His word, God gave them a son.

God really tested this man's faith. Having given Abraham and Sarah this precious gift, God then asked him to choose between his son Isaac and his faith, giving him a fearful direction to sacrifice the boy whom he probably loved more than life itself. Yet his faith in God, and in God's control of his life, never faltered. You can read all the exciting details in *Genesis 22*. God made good on His promise to establish a nation from their offspring, but not at the cost of Isaac's life. Abraham himself would never live to see that promise fulfilled, but he took God at His word, and we read in *Genesis 15* that God credited his faith as righteousness.

There isn't the space here to explore all the other extraordinary examples of faith in *Hebrews 11*, but do please work through them for yourself. We also need to face the fact that these aren't all just simple stories with happy endings. *Hebrews 11:13* brings us smartly back to reality:

These all died in faith, not having received the things promised,
but having seen them and greeted them from afar, and having
acknowledged that they were strangers and exiles on the earth.

In other words the essential nature of faith rewarded in "God's Hall of Faith" is not whether or not these people prospered or lived to receive what God was promising during their time on earth. Some did, and some certainly did not. Faith is never about immediate reward. The real reward of faith was then, as it still remains for us to this day, having a place in the Kingdom of God. There can be no greater reward than to spend eternity with our Lord and Saviour.

What happens when faith fails? **Hebrews 3&4** explores this pertinent but uncomfortable question by examining the exodus; that rather chequered history of God's liberation of the people of Israel from Egyptian slavery. This liberation was also part of God's fulfilment of His promise to Abraham. But what an epic journey it was. Forty years to get from Egypt to the promised land of Canaan! We all know the story, especially the bit about the parting of the Red Sea, and there have been more than a dozen movies made about it. Why was it such an appallingly difficult and slow journey after their miraculous escape from slavery in Egypt? Was God playing an amusing game of celestial snakes and ladders with this unruly bunch of Israelites? There was no lack of snakes disturbing them out in the desert, but no, He certainly wasn't doing that.

What we see in the record of this famous journey, is a persistent failure of faith in God's promise to free them and bring them safely to the land of Canaan, which He had promised would be their permanent home. This was a people who not only wouldn't believe in what they couldn't see, but even doubted what they could see. You might imagine that they would have been totally convinced of the reality of God's presence and protection after seeing the antics of the Egyptian sorcerers and the plagues inflicted on the Egyptians, who endured everything from gnats up their tunics to the wholesale death and destruction which ended with the liberation of the Israelites. And if all that wasn't enough, there was the spectacular miracle of the Red Sea crossing in which they were spared and the pursuing Egyptians perished. Wasn't this all the proof they needed that God was watching over and protecting them? Not a bit of it. All we read are complaints about everything under the sun. They had barely escaped from the oppressive Egyptians who had made their lives so miserable, when they wanted to give up and go back to the very slavery they had complained about. They didn't like the water or the food God provided, and finally thumbed their noses at Moses and at God by setting up a golden idol to worship,and were then punished for their disobedience and lack of faith as *Hebrews 3:19* explains:

> *so we see that they were unable to enter (the promised land) because of unbelief.*

God's response was to delay their entry to Canaan by a whole generation so that it was only their children who would enjoy what God had promised.

The great irony too is that during this whole time the Israelites had the extraordinary witness of the faith of Moses right under their noses. Moses took his stand as one of God's people when he could have lived a life of privilege in the Egyptian royal court. He is described in *Hebrews 11:27* as a man who:

> *...endured as seeing Him who is invisible.*

This is the "eye" of faith again, and through this faith, in his long journey from abandoned child to national leader, he experienced many remarkable examples of God's preservation of Israel detailed in the latter part of **Hebrews 11**.

What is the vital lesson we can learn from these people we read about in God's Hall of Faith? Figures like Abel, Enoch, Noah, Abraham, Moses and the others who appear in Hebrews 11? I think it is this. We really only walk by faith when we genuinely trust that God is ultimately in control of everything we do, and when we look to Him for direction on a day to day basis. This seems simple enough, but I for one know it can be really hard in practice. In my experience there are two particular hazards to watch for.

The first one sneaks up on us when everything in life is going really well. It is the time when we find it just too easy to take God for granted, and we start to ignore His central place in our lives. It mostly happens unconsciously, and we begin to think we can manage life all on our own. Then something goes horribly wrong and suddenly there we are, on our knees and shouting "help" to God. This is usually a moment or a crisis when we realise with a terrible start that we've actually been busy having faith in ourselves and not in Him. I think every Christian is familiar with that experience. It can be very uncomfortable but it should always be an essential spiritual wakeup call.

The second hazard insinuates its way into our thinking very differently. We size up our current situation, mostly when it is one we want to change, and decide by all the logic we can muster, and whatever the prevailing evidence, that we can't or we won't accept that our present situation is what God has planned for us. The core challenge here for every Christian believer is to discern the profound difference between being driven by misdirected human ambition, and being open to making a change which the Lord is guiding. As every mature Christian knows, God's guidance comes in many forms and on many time scales. However it happens, guidance must always start with prayer; firstly that God will strengthen our faith, will deepen our trust and our relationship with Jesus as our Lord and Saviour, and then that we will listen with open hearts and minds to God's guidance and be obedient to it. We cannot expect to hear what God has to tell us unless we start by first asking Him to enrich our relationship and our love for Him, and so prepare us to listen to Him.

If we fail to begin in this way, we risk persisting with our own ambitions which can lead us to actions which at best may be unwise, and at worst may take us beyond the boundaries of acceptable Christian conduct.

There is nothing wrong with having a God-given desire to use the talents He has given us as productively as possible - quite the contrary. Only if we are in a good relationship with him will we readily discern the difference between His ambitions and ours. If we do allow our own ambitions to take over, we risk discontent or even bitter resentment of our current situation. The result is very likely to infect our life of faith and witness and have negative effects not only on us, but those around us as well.

I speak here very much from personal experience. Some years ago I failed to get a position I really wanted, and for three or four months I made myself and everyone around me miserable with my resentment at what I saw as my own failure to achieve what I was certain was the single most important step in my career. I had fallen into the trap that I have just described. It was only when in desperation I handed this burden to God and prayed; "Lord help me accept absolutely that where I am now is where you want me to be", that I had any peace and God lifted the burden from me. And to my great surprise it happened quite quickly, literally one morning as I was driving to work. Did He then immediately proceed to find me a position I liked more? No! He gave me something far better; a sense of contentment that my faltering cry for help to exercise faith in His purposes had been answered. He helped me accept that I was where He wanted me to be at that point in time, and this put me at peace. Long term, it turned out God's future plans for me were very different from mine; but He let me wait another couple of years before I was to discover what they actually were.

There is no evidence in the Bible that we should expect to see faith rewarded here and now with personal success or just getting what we want. On the contrary, God calls some Christians to real, long term personal sacrifice. He calls on some believers to bear burdens and endure suffering that most of us will never understand this side of eternity. So ask yourself, are there things like this in your life that you cannot understand? Things you live with, things that have happened to you that you wish had never occurred? There certainly are in mine, and I am sure that this is true in varying degrees for every last one of us.

Yet our walk of faith should be strong enough to survive the challenges we encounter and be like Job who courageously said in *Job 13:15:*

Though he slay me I will hope in Him.

We need to be like Paul who, after a struggle with what he described as "a thorn in the flesh", simply accepted that God's grace was sufficient for him. We should not expect to demand solutions or explanations as a right. There is only one guarantee, one ultimate reward of faith that God gives us, and that is our place in His Kingdom, just like those in God's Hall of Faith.

I think that part of the problem of this second hazard is the great pressure in our society for us to see success in our Christian lives in the essentially secular terms of immediate reward. Bigger and better houses, more senior jobs, more important leadership roles in our church, you name it. But these are only ever the values of the world, and it is an error leading to nothing but misery if we get seduced into believing we have spiritual rights to success as judged by the world's standards.

As I explained earlier in this chapter, real faith is never our own doing, first and last it is God given. We need to pray every day that He will help us see that the events we are experiencing right now are part of God's purpose for us. St. Paul's arrest in Rome is a great example. Did he sit down and grumble about the injustice of the Roman judicial system? Not at all; instead he saw this as a gospel opportunity. He thanked God for it, seeing it as part of God's plan for him. Read the short letter he wrote to Philemon if you want a graphic illustration of his selfless concern for others during this challenging period of his life, and of his ability to use his situation for the work of God's kingdom. I hope we can all recognise God's hand at work in past events in our lives. We should thank God for that, but it isn't faith, it is an experience of assurance that encourages faith. Recognising the way the hand of God has been at work in our lives is an important experience for every Christian, but it is not faith per se.

We are not lacking for people in our own time who would qualify as examples of the Hall of Faith in *Hebrews 11*. People whose walk of faith has shone brightly even in the most unlikely of circumstances. Gladys Aylward was one such whose story is well known. She was an uneducated working class English parlour maid who was turned down for missionary service in the 1920's when she failed the missionary society examinations. Despite this, Gladys had an unshakeable belief that God was calling her to spread the gospel in China. In 1930, with only a ticket on the trans-Siberian railway and two pounds and ninepence in her pocket, she set out to reach China via Vladivostok. Against all the odds and every bit of prevailing commonsense, she went in faith convinced of God's calling and purposes. Her lifetime of service in China is now one of the modern legends of Gospel ministry.

Not all gospel ministries have results that can be can seen immediately, if at all. Sometimes they seem a bit like God's promises to Abraham, promises which took centuries to be fulfilled. A modern example of this is the several organisations running short wave and internet based gospel broadcasting services across the world. These broadcasts have been really well received for many years, notably in Asia and Africa, but being radio and internet, we will probably never know their full impact. This work continues in faith, because everyone involved believes God has called them to this ministry. The success of this work will never be measured by audience ratings.

We also need to remember that, just as in the days of God's Hall of Faith, it is of no real consequence whether or not our life and our actions square with the expectations of the society in which we live. What matters is to work, with all the diligence we can muster, in whatever ministry we believe God has called us to exercise. Only a God-given faith that is unmoved by the logic and pressures of the world around us can give us the vital spiritual perspective we need to do our part in making this happen.

The latter part of **Hebrews 11** talks of the risks and the terrible suffering experienced by some believers in the past. And these risks remain real today. Now I know that, fortunately, the chances that we will be sawn in two, or forced to clothe ourselves in old goat skins as described in **Hebrews 11**, are probably fairly remote these days. Nevertheless, there are currently at least 50 countries where being a Christian can put your life at risk, or expose you to physical attack or imprisonment. It has been estimated that world wide about a dozen Christians lose their lives for their faith every day. And this is not just my opinion, it is the conclusion independently drawn by international aid organisations and by news agencies like the BBC. A quick internet search will confirm this.

Finally, we need to remember that the principle for which those in the Hall of Faith are commended is the very same principle which holds for us, as **Hebrews 11:39&40** explain:

> *And all these, though commended through their*
> *faith, did not receive what was promised, since God*
> *had provided something better for us, that apart*
> *from us they should not be made perfect.*

In other words, believers both past and present all walk in the same faith. That faith, both for them and for us, leads to Jesus alone as the final fulfilment of God's promise for the return of His Kingdom. As fallen and imperfect people, we are all reconciled with God only through the death and resurrection of Jesus. Jesus is the ultimate, indeed the only, heavenly High priest across all of salvation history. He alone is our spiritual destiny.

In closing our brief look at the question of faith, I would suggest **Hebrews 11:6** as a good starting point for further study, because in many ways it is the key to exploring this chapter in more detail.

> *.....without faith it is impossible to please God, because*
> *anyone who comes to Him must believe that he*
> *exists and that he rewards those who seek Him.*

A daily walk of faith, in which we trust God and His promises first and last, is the key to our relationship with Him, to our understanding the reality of faith, to the assurance of His day to day presence, to our contentment, and ultimately to our confidence of a place in His eternal Kingdom.

Chapter 4
ASSURANCE

T he daily life we lead, at least in the western world, is heavily dependent on the discoveries of science in the past few centuries. Can you imagine a world without electrical power to run everything from trains to telephones, not understanding the chemistry that gives us safe drinking water piped to our houses, or having no access to life-saving drugs? Behind the many discoveries we now regard as essential to modern life, are the remarkable people who made them; and in this chapter I want to look at just two of them, and what shaped their lives.

The first is Michael Faraday, perhaps the most extraordinary genius of them all. He had very little formal education, never went to university, and certainly had no formal training in mathematics or science. Yet his discoveries have made much of the 21st century world as we know it possible. He lived from 1791-1867 and at 14 started work as an apprentice book-binder, a trade which happily gave him an almost unique opportunity to read very widely indeed, and do so without spending a cent. At the end of his seven year apprenticeship in 1812, he went to lectures given by the eminent chemist Sir Humphrey Davy and others, and then proceeded to send Davy a 300 page book of notes he had compiled on his lectures. Impressed by Faraday's efforts, Davy employed him as a lab assistant. Despite his lack of formal education, he had a brilliant inquiring mind and proved to be a meticulous and disciplined experimenter of quite extraordinary ability whose carefully documented investigations in various fields can be read to this day. His discoveries and practical investigations in the fields of electricity and electromagnetism alone have been fundamental to the development of electric motors and generators, and to much of our modern electronics and communications technology, including the cell phones and computers that we now take for granted. Some of the original, and very basic equipment he used for his experiments is still on display at the Royal Institution in London.

The second is James Clerk Maxwell who lived from 1831 to 1879, a Scotsman whose upbringing was in many ways the complete opposite of Faraday's. His parents were well off, and they lived on a 1500 acre estate where the young Maxwell showed a relentless curiosity from an early age about the workings of everything around him. Sadly his mother died when he was only eight, and his early schooling appears to have been rather haphazard. Nonetheless, his potential was recognised, and he was sent to the prestigious Edinburgh Academy where he eventually prospered and made life-long friends. He had wide-ranging interests, which ironically didn't really include passing exams, and wrote his first scientific paper (on geometry) at age fourteen! Leaving the Academy at 16, he went first to Edinburgh University and then later, already a capable mathematician, to Cambridge to complete a further degree in mathematics. He finished his studies in 1854 with great distinction, and went on to lecture at Trinity College Cambridge and then at Marischal College in Aberdeen,

In 1860 he moved to King's College London, where he did research that included pioneering work on colour photography and came in contact with Michael Faraday who was older and already famous. There he also worked on the mathematics of electromagnetism and the polarization of light. Then, after a period as a gentleman scientist on his Scottish estate, he went back to Cambridge as its first Cavendish Professor of Physics and was responsible for establishing its first experimental laboratory that became a famous training ground for aspiring physicists including a string of Nobel laureates. Sadly, he died of cancer at the relatively young age of 48 in 1879.

Of his many contributions to science, perhaps the most famous and wide-ranging in application are what are now known as "Maxwell's Equations". These four equations provide the mathematical basis for all modern electrical engineering and electronics. His work is all the more remarkable because it was published in 1865, well before it found practical application years later in electrical power generation and the radio technology that today underpins things like computer wifi and laptop computers; technology which we now simply take for granted. Of particular importance was Maxwell's work in predicting the existence of electromagnetic (radio) waves well before anyone had worked out how to actually generate them.

A number of present day science historians have remarked on the way Maxwell's contributions to what has become modern electrical engineering complemented the meticulous experimental work of Michael Faraday as he explored the relationships between electricity, magnetism and induction. Then some twenty years later, the German physicist Heinrich Hertz provided the first experimental proof of the existence of radio waves using a very primitive spark transmitter. Based on this research, in 1895 Marconi demonstrated the feasibility of practical radio communications using quite basic equipment which he constructed with the help of the family butler on his father's estate in Italy.

Faraday and Maxwell, one empirical and the other theoretical, were extraordinary geniuses of 19th century science whose impact on our modern world cannot be over-estimated. They also had one other vitally important thing in common. They were both devout Christian believers.

Faraday was a member and eventually an elder, in a small protestant denomination. He lived a quite modest humble life, and despite his enormous international fame, refused a knighthood or other honours, or ever sought to make money from his discoveries. Outside his work as a researcher, he preferred to spend his time active in his church, helping those in need, and retired on a modest pension.

Faraday's assurance about his Christian faith is plain to see in a letter to a Swiss colleague in 1861, six years before his death, where he observed:

> *"Since peace is alone the gift of God, and as it is He who gives it, why should we be afraid? His unspeakable gift in His beloved Son is the ground of no doubtful hope."*

And on his deathbed, when asked what he thought he might be doing in the next world, he replied:

> *"I shall be with Christ, and that is enough"*

Like Faraday, Maxwell enjoyed a great sense of assurance about his Christian faith, and he too was a very humble man who lived out that faith, serving as an elder in his church and spending time visiting the sick and needy. When Maxwell died, one of his academic colleagues at Cambridge observed:

> *"We his contemporaries at college, have seen in him high powers*
> *of mind and great capacity and original views, conjoined with*
> *deep humility before his God, reverent submission to His will, and*
> *hearty belief in the love and atonement of that Divine Saviour*
> *Who was his portion and comforter in trouble and sickness."*

His faith was evident to everyone, in good times and in bad, and demonstrated in his life and actions for all to see.

These men, and others like them, illustrate the important fact that a capacity for original thought is not something you can really just teach people. Education and training can provide us with skills for the life we have chosen, but it cannot guarantee we will make any original contributions to our field of work. They also illustrate the fact that having exceptional intellect capable of outstanding original thinking and also having a lifelong committed Christian faith can co-exist without conflict, and that faith can and should inform and shape our approach to everything that we do. At the end of the day, both faith and intellectual creativity are God-given gifts.

So the big question for us as we look at the strong and unswerving faith of some of these great minds of the past is this: can we be just as certain that our own Christian faith is real, do we share their lifelong confidence in the eternal future which God promises us?

Christians have a thousand and one different stories to tell about how they came to know Jesus as their Lord and Saviour. For many, it was a time of very special experience; suddenly they just knew that God had rescued them from their sin and alienation from Him through the death and resurrection of Jesus.

But then with the passage of time, we know some of these very same people have found their euphoric feeling of certainty giving way to doubt. For some of us, a sense of uncertainty can lead to a real and often intense sense of failure about ourselves, our lives and even faith itself. How much certainty then should we expect to feel about our Christian faith? Should the first warm glow just go on and on? Does doubt, or depression, or our inability to live up to God's standards mean we have somehow failed as a Christian? If we do experience doubt and a sense of failure, does this mean we are missing out on some secret formula for living a victorious Christian life. Or even worse, does it mean there is a risk we will lose our faith altogether?

These are important questions, hard questions, but questions we should, indeed must, explore. They are central to the whole issue of understanding and experiencing Christian assurance. There is no better way to start our exploration than by examining what the Bible has to tell us about assurance, and about the sort of expectations it says we should have concerning the certainty of our Christian faith.

The Bible actually talks about two kinds of assurance. The first is a general sense of assurance about the overall truth and reality of the Gospel, and the second is the personal and individual assurance we should expect to have in our own experience of faith. Let's start with the first one - our general assurance about the reality of the Gospel – although, as we will see, the general and the personal aspects of assurance end up being rather closely intertwined.

Where better to begin than in 1st century Athens, then the intellectual centre of the civilized world. A city famous as a place where there seems to have been no shortage of people eager to hear new ideas and argue about them. Paul's visit there is described in *Acts 17:16-34*, and it is very revealing. He was totally appalled at what he saw. The place was chock full of idols and statues to every so-called god you could think of, and then some. So he started telling people about Jesus and His death and resurrection, beginning as he often did, on home ground in the local synagogue and in the town market place. These were good choices, being locations where there was likely to be an audience. Always being interested to hear new ideas and theories, the locals soon started to take notice. They called him a babbler, and from personal experience I can tell you that academics rarely shy away from blunt and sometimes pretty rude criticism of each other, especially when their comfort zone is being challenged.

We can safely assume there was usually a bit of sledging going on in these public debates, and they soon wanted to hear more from this visiting oddball and his even odder message. So they took Paul off to the Areopagus. I know this sounds a bit like an inner city Greek restaurant, but it was actually a highly influential self appointed public court of intellectuals who liked to sit in judgement on the religious and moral issues of the day. Think of it as a sort of high class first century internet chat room. Paul went straight on the attack, pointing out in *Acts 17* that while they might well be quite religious, they were also quite uncertain what they actually believed. He demonstrated their sense of uncertainty about what gods to believe in by pointing out that they even had an altar inscribed "To an unknown god", just in case they missed one!

Having exposed their underlying spiritual insecurity, Paul then challenged the Athenians in *Acts 17:30&31* with the following claim:

> *"The times of ignorance God overlooked, but*
> *now he commands all people everywhere to*
> *repent, because he has fixed a day on which he*
> *will judge the world in righteousness by a man*

> *whom he has appointed; and of this he has given*
> *assurance to all by raising him from the dead."*

Nor was Paul alone in laying down this sort of challenge. It is repeated by several other writers in the New Testament. For example in **2Peter 1:16–18** the apostle says:

> *"For we did not follow cleverly devised myths when we*
> *made known to you the power and coming of our Lord*
> *Jesus Christ, but we were eyewitnesses of his majesty. For*
> *when he received honor and glory from God the Father,*
> *and the voice was borne to him by the Majestic Glory,*
> *"This is my beloved Son, with whom I am well pleased,"*
> *we ourselves heard this very voice borne from heaven,*
> *for we were with him on the holy mountain."*

Peter writes wanting to assure his readers that the apostles didn't just make all this up. We know the claims of Jesus are real, Peter tells us, because he was there! He is of course referring to the events on the mountain of transfiguration (probably Mount Tabor in modern Israel) which are recorded in the gospels of **Matt 17:5**, **Mark 9:7** & **Luke 9:35**. There, for one heart stopping moment in time, we have an eye-witness account of God Himself directly assuring a small group from the original disciples (Peter, James & John), and who are now apostles, that Jesus really is the Son of God. It's a scene almost beyond our imagination.

Another example is John's assurance in his first epistle which was written to a doubtful and faltering group of Christians in the early church. In his closing verses **1John 5:13** he says:

"I write these things to you who believe in the name of the Son of God that you may know that you have eternal life".

Let me make one essential point here. Personal certainty about being a Christian has to begin by having a general certainty that forgiveness and salvation are only available to us through belief in Jesus Christ and His death and resurrection. The Bible doesn't offer us the option of an intellectual proof that we can just take or leave. Nor does the Bible claim we will be convinced solely by the available historical evidence, and even looking at the wonder of creation isn't enough of itself to assure us that our faith and our salvation are real. Our belief in the reality, in the certainty, and in the assurance that it is possible to be in a saving relationship with the Lord of all creation must begin by acknowledging what God has done for us personally through the life, death and resurrection of Jesus.

We can only do this if we begin by admitting to God that in every respect we fail to meet His standards of holiness, that like the whole human race, we are sinners through and through. This is the only possible starting point. Then we need to acknowledge that we can only be forgiven because Jesus came as God in human form and paid the penalty for our sin by dying on the cross and then rose again having conquered sin and death forever. Very importantly, this can never ever be our own DIY exercise. We can only do this by the power and presence of the Holy Spirit within us. He alone can give us real assured faith that Jesus died and rose again to bring us into an eternal relationship with Him.

The late J.I. Packer, a very gifted British theologian, spoke of the Holy Spirit having a "ministry of illumination" and I think this really captures an essential role He plays in providing us with the experience of assurance when we first come to faith. More than that, His role is absolutely vital in the longer term in sustaining our faith through the ups and downs of life. CS Lewis in "The Screwtape Letters", a book I think should be essential reading for every Christian, talks about "the law of undulation", which is a graphic description of the struggle every Christian experiences of the inevitable tussle between our imperfect and fallen human nature and our spiritually redeemed selves. Truth to tell, none of us would survive as Christians, whether we know it or not, without the power and presence of the Holy Spirit sustaining us through these ups and downs.

This isn't just a New testament thing. **Psalm 62** provides an eloquent reminder that God is the sole source and strength of our faith. **Psalm 19** tells us that even though we can see God's hand in creation and in nature, it is only when God speaks to us through His word and through the work of the Holy Spirit within us, that we can experience faith – or "revival of the soul" as the Psalmist puts it.

And don't discount the supporting evidence about the reality of salvation in Christ seen accumulating in the miraculous life and growth of the early church, evidence we all too easily take for granted. The writer of **Hebrews 2:4** reminds us that:

> *God also bore witness by signs and wonders*
> *and various miracles and by gifts of the Holy*
> *Spirit distributed according to his will.*

This refers to the dramatic evidence of God's saving grace at work recorded in the New Testament, in the establishment and growth of the church. Never under-estimate the miraculous beginnings of the church after Pentecost and the accompanying outpouring of the Holy Spirit. It started as the small, frightened, remnant of an odd little sect in a remote province of the Roman Empire whose leader had just been executed as a common criminal. Yet although they didn't know it, they were on the way to becoming a force that in three centuries time would end up controlling the mighty Roman empire itself. Such an idea would have seemed quite preposterous in first century Judea, but their sometimes semi-literate working class leaders were soon out-arguing the intellectuals and Jewish theologians of the day. They healed people of sickness, they formed religious communities noted for their love and care of its members, they encouraged everyone to join, and they looked after the poor and the elderly.

In short order, they spread the message of Jesus as Saviour all over the civilised world and changed the course of history. And the church today, the people, not the buildings with the stained glass pointy windows, continues to be constant evidence of the grace of God at work. Look no further than St Paul to see the way the early church was an assurance to him and his fellow workers of the reality of what Jesus did for all of us in His death and resurrection. Read his opening comments in his letters to the Christians in Ephesus, Philippi, Colossi, and in Thessaloniki. I'll just quote from the last of these *1Thess 1:2&3:*

> *We (Paul, Silas and Timothy) give thanks to God*
> *always for all of you, constantly mentioning you*
> *in our prayers, remembering before our God and*
> *Father your work of faith and labour of love and*
> *steadfastness of hope in our Lord Jesus Christ"*

Paul and his fellow workers were encouraged and assured of the reality of Christian faith, and what it does to transform individuals and groups of people by the practical outworking of faith, that they saw in the fledgling churches. This was an assurance that faith is real because they could see that it produced real change in real people. We too should be assured by seeing the same things happening in our own congregations and in our wider church. We should be mindful that every time we assemble in the name of Christ we are visible evidence of the reality of God's saving grace at work in the world around us. Taken seriously, that's an awesome responsibility which continues worldwide to this day. Just to take one simple example, over 100 years ago my grandfather and his two brothers-in-law used to meet before work in the bush on the edge of what was then a new suburb in the city of Sydney to pray about establishing a church there. The result more than 100 years on is a vibrant and very active church, surely a tangible example of the reality of faith.

What then of the second aspect, our personal assurance? We need to recognise from the start that God does not promise any of us an earthly rose garden the moment we accept Him as Lord and Saviour and become a Christian. On the contrary, every day we will face a life of challenge in a fallen world where the devil runs rampant; a world that is alien in so many ways to the perfection of God and the standards He sets which we aspire to meet. Make no mistake, this is literally a daily battle, part of the law of undulation I spoke about earlier, and it always will be this side of the grave. Contrary to the opinions of some, there are no magic formulas to escape its challenges. Writing to the church at Ephesus, Paul describes this in dramatic military language. *Ephesians 6:11-13:*

> *Put on the whole armor of God, that you may be able*
> *to stand against the schemes of the devil. For we do not*
> *wrestle against flesh and blood, but against the rulers,*
> *against the authorities, against the cosmic powers over*

this present darkness, against the spiritual forces of evil in the heavenly places. Therefore take up the whole armor of God, that you may be able to withstand in the evil day, and having done all, to stand firm.

You get this very same message from Peter in his first epistle where he calls the devil a roaring lion looking for people to devour.

So recognise from the start that, in every one of our lives, the struggle against evil, the struggle within each one of us against the wrongdoing that is part of our fallen nature, is a real and an absolutely normal experience for every Christian. A rose garden it is not.

In our fallen world, sometimes life can and does go wrong for all of us. Yet if we have accepted Jesus as our Saviour, God in His mercy forgives our all too frequent human failures. There's a spectacular example of this recorded in **Matthew 26:69-75** where we find Peter sitting in the courtyard of the High Priest's house while Jesus is inside on trial for His life. Peter is challenged as being a follower and vehemently denies it, beats a retreat to the front of the house, and gets challenged there again. He repeats his denial and curses. Then the dreadful realisation of what he has done dawns on him and he is utterly crushed. Does this sound familiar? Jesus knew this man would falter and told him so, and yet this pathetic weeping figure is the very same man that God in His infinite grace and mercy used to become one of the great leaders of the New Testament church. I doubt we will ever fully understand the quite extraordinary extent of God's measureless grace this side of eternity, but experiencing it and seeing it at work in others is central to having real assurance about the reality of our faith in what God has done for us in Christ.

We should take heart from the fact that the early church was full of ordinary fallible people just like you and me. There are examples everywhere in the epistles. Paul warned the church at Corinth about divisiveness in *1Cor 1:10*, he warned the church in Galatia about following false teaching in *Gal 1:16*, and he gently admonished folk in the church at Philippi about feuding with each other in *Phil 4:2*. If you want more, look in the epistles of Peter, James and John. All the common pitfalls caused by human frailty which we face today can be seen there!

Because we fail it doesn't mean we should simply give up. On the contrary. I've laboured this point for one crucially important reason: if we have unrealistic expectations about our Christian faith, and expect that we will be perfect from day one, if we expect our church leaders always to be textbook examples of faith, then I guarantee we'll be disappointed. If our expectations are unrealistic, then we are also far more likely to have serious doubts about our faith than if we accept the reality that this side of heaven nobody is perfect, not a single one of us. We all fail, we all get things wrong. Our assurance must come from knowing that if we acknowledge our constant shortcomings, God goes on forgiving us, and if we acknowledge that failure every time, He will gently put us back on our feet to fight the next battle. Each time this happens we should expect to meet the challenges of life with an increased trust in Him. We only win our battles, we only learn, and we only grow in faith when we meet our challenges in God's strength.

At one extreme, does this mean we can exploit God's grace? Is it a licence to run amok and then beg forgiveness on a regular basis (rage on Saturdays, and confess on Sundays)? Absolutely not! A key outcome of our daily battle must be visible change when we confess Christ as Lord because the Holy Spirit is at work within us even if we can't see it. Paul says to the Galatians in *Gal 5:22-23*:

...the fruit of the spirit is love, joy, peace, patience, kindness, goodness, faithfulness, gentleness, self-control.

Despite our imperfect nature, these are the qualities that should be seen, and seen to grow in us. They are a vital part of Christian assurance that our faith is real. The message here is not to rely on inner feelings. In varying degrees we all have emotional ups and downs, and they don't make a reliable spiritual barometer. Our actions, our priorities, and our daily stumbling attempts to live to God's standards are far more telling.

We shouldn't forget either, that it is not unusual to have fears that our faith will fail altogether. But God has anticipated this, and the Bible has great promises for us, and they are put there to lay those fears to rest. Jesus says in *John 6:39,40:*

And this is the will of him who sent me, that I should lose nothing of all that he has given me, but raise it up on the last day. For this is the will of my Father, that everyone who looks on the Son and believes in him should have eternal life, and I will raise him up on the last day.

And again in *John 10:27,28:*

My sheep hear my voice, and I know them, and they follow me. I give them eternal life, and they will never perish, and no one will snatch them out of my hand.

Paul, ever the lawyer, in *Romans 8:35&37* spells out in fine detail the comprehensive nature of God's assurance that He will preserve our faith. It reads like a well drafted contract designed to cover all the bases.

Who shall separate us from the love of Christ? Shall tribulation, or distress, or persecution, or famine, or nakedness, or danger, or sword? As it is written, "For your sake we are being killed all the day long; we are regarded as sheep to be slaughtered." No, in all these things we are more than conquerors through him who loved us. For I am sure that neither death nor life, nor angels nor rulers, nor things present nor things to come, nor powers, nor height nor depth, nor anything else in all creation, will be able to separate us from the love of God in Christ Jesus our Lord.

This has been a pretty wide-ranging discussion that has taken us from the lives of 19th century scientists to Paul's detailed letter to the church in Rome, so let me try and summarise the ground we've covered.

I believe our personal sense of assurance about our faith depends on at least three key things.

- We must acknowledge that the death and resurrection of Jesus is the only means by which anyone can have faith and forgiveness for all our failures, and must recognise that this faith comes only through the work of the Holy Spirit within us.
- We must recognise that we won't ever find the walk of faith easy, it will always be a daily challenge. We mustn't rely on our feelings, we must look to God constantly for His help and His presence.
- We must understand that if our faith is real, God's standards must be seen by others in our lives and in the way we treat people around us.

I think we can see these qualities in the lives of Faraday and Maxwell. They were brilliant men with intellects the like of which most us can barely comprehend, but their faith and trust in Jesus as their Saviour was exactly the same as for all the rest of us. Despite their status in the scientific community, they still found the time to provide practical love and care for people in need in their community, just as Jesus tells us we should. This concern for the welfare of others was a great marker of the reality of their faith and trust in Him, and so it should be for us.

Finally, no matter who we are, no matter what our status, we must share a common confidence with all our fellow believers that even if the roof seems to be falling in on us, we can still trust that God remains in ultimate control and remains true to His promise that He will not let us out of His hand, ever!

Let me finish with a conversation held in December 1784, four years before the first fleet sailed into Sydney harbour, because I think it says it all. The speakers are two famous evangelical Christians, John Wesley the missionary and famous 18th century revival preacher, and Charles Simeon, the Rector for 50 sometimes turbulent years of Holy Trinity church Cambridge.

Simeon says to Wesley *"Allowing then, that you were first turned by the grace of God, are you not in some way to keep yourself by your own power?"*

"No," says Wesley

"What then?" says Simeon *"are you to be upheld every hour and every moment by God, as much as an infant in its mother's arms?"*

"Yes, altogether," says Wesley

"And is all your hope in the grace and mercy of God to preserve you to His heavenly kingdom?" asks Simeon

"Yes" says Wesley, *"I have no hope, but in Him"*

It is the recognition that we are ultimately and absolutely in God's care which is the ultimate source of all our Christian assurance. If you have not experienced this, I urge you to pray right now confessing your failures and asking God to forgive all your sins and short-comings, asking that through the death and resurrection of Jesus, He will take you and keep you forever in His care.

Finally, as Christian believers, we would all do well to pray with writer of **Psalm 71**

> *O God, from my youth you have taught me, and I still proclaim your wondrous deeds. So even to old age and gray hairs, O God, do not forsake me, until I proclaim your might to another generation, your power to all those to come.*

Chapter 5
DOUBT

There's an old story about a murder trial in which overwhelming circumstantial evidence was presented against the accused, but there was also a big problem: the body of the victim had never been found. The slick defence attorney was desperate to get his client, the accused, acquitted. So in the best tradition of popular TV dramas he strode dramatically up and down in front of the jury as he made his closing arguments, knowing full well he was on pretty thin ice. He also knew that without the evidence of an actual dead body, he still had a fair chance of getting his client acquitted, just on the basis of doubt.

As he was making his final pitch, he had a sudden inspiration. He stopped, spun around and addressed the judge directly, saying: "Your Honour, in ten seconds the alleged murder victim will walk in through those doors behind us!" The jury of course was absolutely stunned, and they all turned and stared at the courtroom doors. There was a short but dramatic silence, then the defense attorney hooted with laughter saying

"Ha! I just made that up! But you all looked at the doors. You obviously at least half expected to see the alleged victim walk in, so you're not really certain there has been a murder at all!" You can only imagine the uproar in the court that followed.

When everyone had calmed down, the slick defence attorney approached the judge and said "Your Honour, I demand this case be dismissed. How can someone be accused of murder when no body has been found, and while I admit the alleged victim seems to have disappeared, there's no actual evidence of a murder. If that isn't enough, you just saw me prove that the jury has genuine doubts the alleged victim is really actually dead!" It was all pretty sensational.

The jury retired to consider the evidence, and then returned to the courtroom quite quickly with a verdict of "guilty". The defence attorney was totally astonished he thought his courtroom performance had been quite brilliant, especially the last bit, and was quite confident that his client would simply be acquitted. So he said to the jury foreman, "How could you possibly convict my client? You all immediately looked at the courtroom doors when I said the victim would walk in. You all really thought he might just appear as I suggested. You had real doubts!"

"Yes", said the jury foreman, "It's true, we did look at the doors, but we also looked at your client, the accused. He didn't so much as move a muscle, let alone look at the doors. He wasn't expecting anyone!"

Doubt comes in many different forms and although it sometimes gets a bad press, it can also be a good thing. In the story I just recounted, doubt came from a very understandable lack of proof, despite highly suspicious circumstances, that a murder had actually been committed. That doubt vanished when it became obvious from his reactions that the chief suspect evidently seemed to know that the alleged victim really was dead.

We sometimes need to start with doubt to get to actual truth, which is perhaps why the English philosopher Francis Bacon, often called the father of scientific method, said:

> *"If a man will begin with certainties, he shall end in doubts; but if he will be content to begin with doubts, he shall end in certainties."*

This is a view which also fits well with German philosopher and theologian Paul Tillich's observation that: *"Doubt isn't the opposite of faith; it is an element of faith."*

And perhaps it is one reason for Bram Stoker, the creator of Dracula, observing that: *"We learn from failure, not from success!"*

It is evident that doubt and healthy scepticism have played a significant part in the evolution of modern scientific inquiry and its methodologies over the past 500 years or more. But understanding the world we live in isn't driven by this alone. Can you imagine living in a world defined only by doubt? The Danish philosopher and theologian Soren Kierkegaard wrestled with this issue and concluded that: *"Every mental act is composed of doubt and belief, but it is belief that is the positive, it is belief that sustains thought and holds the world together."*

Against these rather diverse views on doubt that seem to have prevailed for centuries, we can really only get a properly Christian perspective on how doubt should fit into our world view if we begin with an understanding of the reaction Jesus had to doubt and how it might affect believers.

Doubt from any perspective is an important issue because it is a very common experience, even amongst mature Christians of longstanding faith. Unsurprisingly therefore, it is one of the many weapons Satan tries to use to undermine our faith. Fortunately, we know from the gospel record that Jesus really understood this problem, and we can see a good example of Him handling doubt when we examine the events of *Matthew 11:1-3:*

> *When Jesus had finished instructing his twelve disciples,*
> *he went on from there to teach and preach in their cities.*
> *Now when John heard in prison about the deeds of the*
> *Christ, he sent word by his disciples and said to him, "Are*
> *you the one who is to come, or shall we look for another?"*

The background to this is that Jesus had been teaching in the towns of Galilee. John meantime, had been imprisoned by Herod Antipas in the desolate mountain fortress of Machaerus east of the Dead Sea for his outspoken criticism of Herod's evil regime, and especially about the questionable morality of his marriage. John's particular crime had been to denounce Herod's marriage as contrary to Jewish law, which was a public censure the despot Herod just couldn't tolerate. It has been observed by historians that the Herods of this period were not a nice lot. His father Herod the Great was a particularly dreadful man, and totally paranoid about rivals. Nobody who even potentially might be a threat to him was safe, including his own family. The Emperor Caesar Augustus apparently once joked that it was safer to be Herod's pig than to be one of his sons! This was rather ironic given that eating pork was contrary to Jewish law anyway.

Hearing from prison about Jesus' ministry in Galilee, John is recorded in both *Matt 11* and *Luke 7* telling his disciples to go and ask Jesus if He really was the Messiah, or If they should they wait and expect someone else?

Now I have often wondered why on earth John of all people asked this question? We know from the gospel record that John not only knew exactly who Jesus was, but that he also clearly understood his own role as the herald of Jesus' coming. The gospel of Mark records this in **Mark 1:9-11:**

In those days Jesus came from Nazareth of Galilee and was baptized by John in the Jordan. And when he came up out of the water, immediately he saw the heavens being torn open and the Spirit descending on him like a dove. And a voice came from heaven, "You are my beloved Son; with you I am well pleased."

John clearly knew that his role was simply to announce the coming of the Messiah. In **John 1:34** he says outright that he knows this is the Son of God, and he obviously had a keen interest in what Jesus went on to do. Why then this question?

Had his imprisonment made him doubt his own role as the herald for Jesus, and then doubt that Jesus was the Promised One? Was he disappointed in the kind of ministry that Jesus had conducted? Was he uncomfortable because Jesus mixed with undesirables like Matthew the tax collector? Was he sceptical because Jesus didn't fast or share his very austere lifestyle? Was he like so many Jews of the time, deeply resentful of Roman occupation and expecting a very different all con-quering Messiah who would miraculously restore the political and spir-itual fortunes of Israel? Maybe Jesus just didn't fit his preconceived ideas about the long expected Messiah. Or, as he faced his own certain death, was this simply a "Dorothy Dix" question asked just to reassure his own disciples?

Whatever the explanation, this episode illustrates that the problem of doubt is nothing new for believers, not even for someone like John the Baptist. Jesus responded to the inquiry from John's disciples with a simple answer as **Matt 11:4-6** records.

> **And Jesus answered them, "Go and tell John what you hear and see: the blind receive their sight and the lame walk, lepers are cleansed and the deaf hear, and the dead are raised up, and the poor have good news preached to them. And blessed is the one who is not offended by me."**

At first reading this might sound like Jesus just trying to promote Himself. But far from it, He's actually referring directly to Isaiah's prophesy about the miraculous events which would accompany the coming of the Kingdom of God in the person of Jesus. You can read this for yourself in **Isaiah 35:4-6 & 61:1,2**. Jesus is simply reassuring John that His ministry is actually fulfilling Isaiah's prophesy. And He ends in verse 6 with a gentle reminder to John that all who have faith in Him will be blessed.

In effect, Jesus is telling John and his followers not to have preconceived ideas about His ministry. He didn't come, as many hoped, perhaps even John, to liberate the Jews from Roman occupation. He didn't come to be another John the Baptist living a life of self denial in the desert. He came to minister to the poor, to heal the sick, to engage with ordinary people, including some quite disreputable characters, and most importantly of all He came to bring sinners back to God, redeemed by His death and resurrection.

Nor does it end there. He came to bring the message of salvation not just to the Jews, but to the whole gentile world and by doing this, to prepare the world for His final triumphant return to rule over His creation. So in answering John's question, He's asking them to look beyond popular preconceptions about the Messiah and see not only what He has done, but that in His actions, He is actually fulfilling Old Testament prophesy.

Not content with dispelling John's doubts, Jesus then goes on to explain to the crowd who had been following Him just where John himself fits in, and perhaps until now even John himself hadn't fully understood the significance of his own ministry, even though it had actually been quite sensational. Thousands had flocked to hear him and to be baptised by this way-out hippy living a very alternative desert life-style, surviving on simple bush tucker. In a time of Roman oppression, a time of very politicised and legalistic religion, John called for national repentance and baptism, which infuriated the religious establishment of the day. Even more provocatively, he had gone on to claim, quite correctly, to be the herald of the Messiah who would judge and rule the world.

So it's appropriate, with doubt in the air, for Jesus to explain John's role before his imprisonment to a wider audience in *Matt 11:7-10.*

As they went away, Jesus began to speak to the crowds concerning John: "What did you go out into the wilderness to see? A reed shaken by the wind? What then did you go out to see? A man dressed in soft clothing? Behold, those who wear soft clothing are in kings' houses. What then did you go out to see? A prophet? Yes, I tell you, and more than a prophet. This is he of whom it is written, Behold, I send my messenger before your face, who will prepare your way before you."

In verse 7, after John's disciples had left, Jesus asks the people what they came out in the desert to see. Was it a weak and uncertain man? Obviously not, because John was clearly strong and fearless . Was it to see a man dressed in fashionable clothing? Obviously not, John wore a very simple tunic made of camel hair. Was it to hear a prophet speak?

Yes of course. But much more than an ordinary prophet. Jesus quotes **Malachi 3:1** to them because his prophesy refers to John the Baptist and his special role.

> *Behold, I send my messenger, and he will prepare the way before me. And the Lord whom you seek will suddenly come to his temple; and the messenger of the covenant in whom you delight, behold, he is coming, says the LORD of hosts.*

Jesus identifies John as the greatest and the last in the long line of prophets who appear in salvation history. His job in one way was simple enough: he was there to announce that God's covenant promise of a Messiah was now being fulfilled once and for all time. So here's a neat twist; John's ministry serves firstly as an assurance that Jesus really is who He claims to be, and secondly, when John asks Jesus for assurance, He tells John to look at his own unique ministry, because that itself has fulfilled some of the key Old Testament prophesy about the coming of the Messiah.

We should be greatly encouraged by the way Jesus treated John's doubt. There is nothing defensive, dismissive, or rude in Jesus' reply to John. On the contrary, His response is patient and very constructive. John and his followers are encouraged to look at the evidence of Jesus' ministry, and to see the way that it fulfills Old Testament prophesy, and not to be distracted by personality or style, or any contemporary preconceptions about the promised Messiah. Jesus' response is simply designed to encourage faith, to remind everyone what prophets like Isaiah and others have long had to say about the promised Messiah, and never to belittle the questioner. His whole approach was to dispel doubt by helping his questioners understand what God had explained and recorded in His Word.

As we explore the whole question of doubt, we also need to recognise that it comes in a number of forms. John's question is an example of "propositional doubt". He's not actually flat out denying who Jesus is; he's only expressing uncertainty. He really just wants to know, has he got it right? This sort of doubt is not uncommon in the Bible, and it is not uncommon for believers in every age in their daily walk with the Lord.

We can't talk about doubt without of course mentioning that most famous of all doubters, Thomas. In **John 14** Jesus starts preparing His disciples for His earthly departure, explaining that He must now go to His Father so that they can eventually join Him there in eternity. From their reactions, what He said was clearly but predictably hard for them to fathom at that point in time. It is Thomas who has the courage to express their doubts when he says in **John 14:5:**

> *"Lord we do not know where you are going.*
> *How can we know the way?"*

Jesus gives them that most wonderful, loving, reassuring and famously definitive of answers in **John 14:6&7:**

> *"I am the way and the truth and the life. No one*
> *comes to the Father except through me. If you really*
> *knew me, you would know my Father as well. From*
> *now on, you do know him and have seen him."*

After the resurrection, it was Thomas again who was very vocal in doubting what the others had reported. He said he wanted to feel the actual wounds Jesus had suffered on the cross before he could really believe Jesus had risen. So when Jesus appeared again to His disciples, as *John 20:27* records, He went straight up to Thomas and without rebuke simply invited him to feel the wounds in His hands and His side. Thomas's reaction was immediate. Falling at the feet of Jesus he declares *"My Lord and my God!"*. This is "provisional doubt". He didn't deny outright that Jesus had risen, but he wanted evidence to allay his doubts.

Doubt can also take the more dangerous form of outright denial. This was the approach Satan used in persuading Eve to disobey God in the Garden of Eden. The well known author Somerset Maugham said *"I do not believe in God, I see no need of such an idea."* This is doubt which directly denies the existence of God and therefore who Jesus is. Doubt like this doesn't seek answers, it is just outright disbelief, and it has fatal consequences. It directly rejects God and His offer of grace to a fallen world in sending Jesus. It simply and tragically rejects His offer of salvation.

Almost everybody experiences doubt at one time or another. Not necessarily doubt that denies God's existence, but more the "what if" kind of doubt that John the Baptist and Thomas experienced. There are many examples of this in the Bible: Moses, Gideon, Elijah, Jonah, and Peter to name but some. Let me look at just one of these, the extraordinary story of Gideon who is a prime example of stubbornly persistent provisional doubt. Doubt that was overcome by God's grace and supreme patience in the face of evidence which should have dispelled doubt very early in the story. His saga of doubt begins in *Judges 6* where we find the people of Israel under God's judgement for serial disobedience to Him, the one who had rescued them from the Egyptians and sustained them in their long desert odyssey. It seems that as God's people the Israelites had very short memories when it came to trusting God and their favoured place in His creation.

As a punishment for their faithless embrace of pagan Caananite religions, God allowed the Midianites and other neighbouring tribes to raid them, laying waste to their crops and livestock and forcing their retreat to caves in the mountains. Things got pretty desperate, and eventually, as in time past, they cried out to God to rescue them. We first meet Gideon as he encounters an angel of God who appears while he's threshing wheat in, of all things, a wine-press to try and hide it from the Caananite raiders. The angel assures him he is a mighty man of valor and that God is with him. Gideon is rather sceptical, and asks, if this is true, why is Israel being ruined by raiders, why don't they see the hand of the Lord protecting them, as in earlier times? The angel just tells him to go and save Israel. Gideon protests that he doesn't have the military capability to fight the Midianites but the angel assures him that in God's strength he can do it. Still unconvinced, Gideon insists on the angel waiting while he prepares a sacrificial offering, demanding a sign from the angel. The offering includes bread, the meat of a sacrificial goat and a bowl of soup made from the said goat. The angel then directs Gideon to put the offering on a rock and pour the soup over the meat and the bread. The angel touches this offering with his staff, it is immediately consumed by fire, and the angel promptly vanishes.

Gideon wanted a sign and he certainly got one. Can you imagine trying to set fire to the Sunday roast and a loaf of bread after first pouring a whole bowl of soup over them? Suitably impressed by his heavenly visitor, he built an altar there to the Lord who that same night went on to direct him to demolish the main town altar to Baal and other buildings dedicated to Caananite gods and replace them with an altar to the Lord. Gideon did as he was asked, but being naturally timid did it all at night for fear of retribution from townspeople and the rest of his family. Unsurprisingly there was outrage when Gideon's handiwork was revealed, and the townsfolk wanted to lynch him. Gideon's father Joash defended his son, telling them all that, if Baal was real, then this god would deal with Gideon himself. Even so there was a gathering of tribes opposing Israel in the Jezreel Valley, a fertile plain west of the Jordan River and it wasn't for a friendly visit.

At this point two very interesting things happened. The Spirit of the Lord came upon Gideon, and our reluctant hero was transformed into a leader who proceeded to summon help from several surrounding Hebrew tribes. You might imagine that by now Gideon would be fully confident of God's presence and protection, but alas no. He still had doubts and wanted more proof that God's promise first delivered by the angel was really true, which brings us to the famous, perhaps infamous, fleece test. Wanting more proof, Gideon laid a fleece on a dry floor telling God he would believe His promise if overnight the fleece would become wet while the floor remained dry. Sure enough, next morning the fleece alone was soaking wet. Was Gideon convinced of God's intentions? Not a bit of it! His reaction was to ask God not to be angry, but that, just to be sure, please this time could He keep the fleece dry and make the floor wet. In His infinite love and patience God did exactly that. Gideon had surely tested God's patience, and now it seems it was His turn to test Gideon. Over 30,000 people had assembled to support Gideon in the impending battles with the horde of soldiers from hostile Caananite tribes currently assembled in the Jezreel Valley. God told Gideon that with so many people assembled He wouldn't act against the Midianites and their fellow invaders in case the Israelites then boasted they had saved themselves. God then instructed Gideon to tell anyone fearful about the impending battle to go home. That left an army of some 10,000, and God said this was still too big, so by testing the way they drank water, the Israelite battle group was whittled down to a mere 300. Then if they won the battle with such a small number, nobody could possibly doubt it had been a God-given miracle.

What then followed amounted to psychological warfare. Gideon made a secret night reconnaissance to the huge Midianite camp where he overheard a conversation between two soldiers which indicated they were terrified and expected to lose the forthcoming battle with the Israelites. Gideon returned to his own camp now quite assured that God would make his army victorious. The plan was simple enough and worked well. The 300 men set off with their swords, torches hidden inside clay jars, and trumpets. They went at night by stealth into the Midianite camp and on Gideon's signal broke their clay jars which were hiding the light of their torches, and blew their trumpets shouting, "A sword for the Lord and for Gideon". This frightened the living daylights out of the huge army assembled in the Jezreel valley and they fled, pursued by Gideon's full army who also recaptured land previously occupied by the invaders.

This is an extraordinary story of doubt being transformed into trust through the promise of an extraordinary miracle , and all achieved by the patient outworking of the grace of God. Patience that Gideon really tested, but patience which was not wasted, because he then went on to serve the Lord faithfully for a lifetime. This story is certainly not an encouragement to test God's patience, but it does remind us of His seemingly inexhaustible graciousness toward us when we genuinely struggle with doubt.

I would really encourage readers to explore other examples like these for yourselves and see the way God has dealt patiently and wisely with people struggling with faith and how He has cared for them. It is one good way of learning more about the depth and breadth of God's grace to us all. Doubt is often part of our journey to faith in the first place, and then becomes part of our ongoing walk of faith.

Sometimes doubt is triggered by tragedy or illness or some other unexpected and catastrophic event in our lives which brings on doubt that makes us ask "God, why have you let this happen to me? Do you really care about me?" Sometimes it is less a problem of belief and more a problem of choice; a question of uncertainty about what God wants us to do with our lives. It might be a time when faith just seems out and out confusing, and we really can't understand how God's purposes are working for us. It might be part of a time when our relationship to God seems distant and uncertain.

So what does the Bible teach us about dealing with doubt? The first thing to get quite clear is that God does not just condemn us for struggling with doubts. The second is that the Bible makes it plain that God is very patient with genuine inquiring doubters, and, when we ask, He is always generous in providing us with assurance that is appropriate to our situation. We serve a God who understands us and our human frailty far better than we will ever know this side of heaven. He doesn't hold back in dealing with doubt. John the Baptist's own ministry as we saw earlier was validated by Jesus in His response to John's doubt, and Thomas was confronted with the most complete and intimate physical evidence possible of the reality of Jesus's death and resurrection. Gideon's demands for proof of the truth of God's intentions were to say the least exorbitant, yet God dealt with him patiently and grew Gideon's faith mightily in the process.

If we are experiencing doubts, the very worst thing we can do is to try and resolve them on our own just because we feel too guilty to bring them before God Himself. This only ever makes things worse, and is likely to leave us with more, not less, uncertainty. Faith is God's great gift to us, as Paul reminds us in **Ephesians 2**, and it only comes by the work of the Holy Spirit within us and never ever by our own efforts.

The only right response to doubt is to bring every last bit of uncertainty and fear that we may be experiencing before the Lord Himself. We need to ask for His grace and mercy in resolving whatever is causing our doubts, and this always needs to start with the repair and enriching of our personal relationship with Him. The evidence of scripture is very clear: God responds generously when we call on Him and Him alone. Paul writes in **Romans 8:38&39:**

> *For I am sure that neither death nor life,*
> *nor angels nor rulers, nor things present nor things*
> *to come, nor powers, nor height nor depth, nor*
> *anything else in all creation, will be able to separate*
> *us from the love of God in Christ Jesus our Lord.*

We need to claim that wonderful promise very single day.

And finally, there is a flipside to all this. As believers we all have a continuing pastoral responsibility to support and care for our brothers and sisters in Christ when they struggle with doubt. **Jude 21&22** tells us:

> *Keep yourselves in the love of God, waiting for the*
> *mercy of our Lord Jesus Christ that leads to eternal*
> *life. And have mercy on those who doubt.*

Paul gives us the same message in **Romans 14**, namely to look after those experiencing doubt. No matter how imperfectly, we should aim to show anyone struggling with doubt the same love, mercy, patience and grace that God constantly shows to us. It's all too easy to fall into the trap of intolerance and judgement of our fellow believers who are struggling with doubt. Their struggle today could just as easily be ours tomorrow.

We need to pray every day that the Lord will bless us and keep us close as we walk with Him, perhaps sometimes doubting, but within the limits of our frail human nature always seeking His assurance as we try in our lives to imitate His immeasurable love in sending us Jesus to be our Lord and Saviour and as we encourage others in their daily walk with Him.

Chapter 6
TRUST

H ere you are, sitting in the smoking ruin of your burnt out six bedroom mansion. It is a freezing cold winter's day, drizzling, there are mounds of rubbish and ash everywhere, rats are scurrying around, and all you are wearing is a dirty old blanket scrounged from a nearby wheelie bin. Your designer clothes have all gone, thieves have stolen your brand new Mercedes, your four wheel drive, and your speedboat . Your trusted family accountant has embezzled your life savings, and it gets worse. Your credit cards and bank accounts have all been frozen, your business is bankrupt, and members of your family have been abducted by a terrorist. Then, to add to this litany of misery, you have broken out in painful oozing boils everywhere making you look and feel disgusting. To top it all off, your wife, with whom you have enjoyed a happy marriage for many years, has just left telling you to curse God and drop dead. In short, your life is a complete train wreck.

You try to get a bit of relief as you sit in the wreckage of your once comfortable home by scratching yourself on all the itchiest parts with a broken dinner plate, and as you sit there, you wonder just how and why all this could possibly have happened. Then a bunch of so-called friends rock up in a fancy convertible, and after a long silence while they just stare at your terrible and almost unrecognisable state, these itinerant wiseguys have the gall to tell you at interminable length that this is all your fault!

An unlikely story? Perhaps not as unlikely as you might at first think. This is a possible modern TV series version of Job's story in the Old Testament. **Job** is a really hard book. Hard, because it confronts us, warts and all, with the problem of human suffering, and more than that with the puzzle of apparently undeserved suffering. Those of us who live in safe western countries are mostly protected from extreme scenarios like Job's unless we have experienced a major flood or bushfire. But in parts of the Middle East, in Africa and more recently in the Ukraine, there are many people, often through no fault of their own, who have suddenly found themselves in just such a situation. Homeless, bombed out of their houses, everything they had owned and cherished destroyed, financially ruined, and in some cases injured or even killed. All this often as innocent bystanders who have become part of the collateral damage of war, terrorism, religious intolerance, local politics, or natural disasters like floods, fires, earthquakes, and the Covid pandemic.

Since the start of the present millennium alone, whole towns and cities in parts of the Middle East, Africa and the Ukraine have been reduced to unlivable rubble, leaving millions homeless with no access to clean water, no sewage, no electricity and no shelter, let alone any semblance of proper housing. Many have only been able to find sustainable accommodation by joining one of the huge refugee camps that have been set up in these regions of the world. According to international aid agencies such as the UNHCR, as at the end of 2022, over 100 million people have had to flee from their homes because of various conflicts and disasters. So it comes as no surprise that some of the camps are the size of cities, housing anywhere from fifty to over one hundred thousand people, many of whom end up staying there for years. You can see the scale of the problem for yourself from aerial pictures that are readily found on Google Earth.

It might be uncomfortable, but we can't escape the fact that we live in a world where terrible things just keep on happening, often to folk just going about their daily business. And we ask ourselves, why is it that one person dies in an industrial accident, or from a terrorist bomb, or a plane crash, while other people nearby survive? Job is asking the same sort of question. Why me? He wants to know why his life has suddenly become a disaster. Why, when he was living a quiet, comfortable, orderly and peaceful family life, has a series of catastrophic events all but destroyed him? That's the challenge which confronts Job as he tries to make some sense of the disastrous situation which has overtaken him.

The book opens with God putting the basic proposition to Satan that, come what may, Job is a righteous man through and through and will remain so whatever happens to him, and not, as Satan argues, just because he was happy, healthy and well off.

Job is a daunting book because its 42 chapters seem to go on forever, and we certainly can't explore all of it here. However, it is well worth trying to understand its basic structure and message, or otherwise you could be forgiven for not feeling like reading it at all. And that would be a pity, because it contains some great lessons for us. In broad outline, it runs this way:

In Chapters 1 & 2 God and Satan argue about Job. The scene is set, and Job is stripped of everything he has, including his health, and he is tested literally to within an inch of death. But even though his life is all but completely destroyed, he doesn't blame God. And importantly, he rejects his wife's unhelpful call in *Job 2:9* to:

"*curse God and die*".

As we shall see, for all his misery Job's fears lie elsewhere.

Then his three friends appear, Eliphaz, Bildad and Zophar. They are so aghast at his appearance and his misery, that they sit in absolute silence with him for a whole week. Can you imagine a whole week of silence? Could any of us actually do that? Truth to tell, most of us aren't very good at even a day of silence! And why a week? The seven days of silence are actually very significant, because this is the traditional interval of time in Hebrew culture for mourning the dead. Not an encouraging sign for Job though, but that's how they saw him, as good as dead.

After this ritual silence we quickly discover that these felllows could talk under wet cement and they are all very different, although not always in a good way! Eliphaz is the nicest and gentlest of the three, he has more insight than the others, and he approaches Job as a good man who has just gone a bit astray. Bildad by contrast is a tough legalistic scholar not given to much sympathy. He thinks Job's questioning of the justice of what God has allowed to happen is blasphemous, and that Job and his family have got what they deserved. Finally there's Zophar who thinks he knows it all when really he's a bit of a prat. He's a man without compassion, much given to theorising, and his rather unhelpful advice to Job is to repent or die.

Then later, another guy appears. Elihu. Young, impatient, and rather self important. He talks a lot, not always really saying very much. However in spite of that, he actually has some real insights into Job's situation.

So from *Job 4-37* (I told you they could talk under wet cement) these fellows give Job a lot of mostly unhelpful advice, and certainly offer him no real comfort in his present distress. After each has spoken, Job replies to them. Then eventually, God talks directly with Job and everything is finally resolved.

Job 3 sets the basic scene. Before his friends get started on him, all the misery just floods out of poor old Job. He is so desperately unhappy that he wishes he had never been born, and he goes on at some length about this. Again, he never actually blames God for his situation, and by the end of the chapter it emerges that his real fear is something he has always dreaded: that somehow he has lost God's favour. Here is a man in acute pain and misery, totally bewildered and almost destroyed by what has happened to him; and he is desperately looking for answers.

As I mentioned at the start, there's more in this book than we can deal with in just one short chapter, so I want to focus mostly on *Job 11*. Eliphas and Bildad have had their first say, and now comes Zophar who wades into Job with all the subtlety of a brick in a glasshouse.

He begins in *Job 11:2&3* by first accusing Job of too much idle talk. And yes, Job has certainly had a lot to say, he's possibly been a bit over the top, but this is just Job's natural human emotion overflowing as he expresses his grief and complete bewilderment at his situation. He's convinced, for reasons he simply cannot understand, even though he desperately wants to, that God is angry with him. He has steadfastly maintained his own innocence as he says in *Job 9:21:*

"I am blameless; I regard not myself; I loathe my life."

Despite his present predicament, he doesn't ask God to restore his fortunes, he doesn't abuse or blame God, and he doesn't claim to be perfect. As he addresses God in *Job 7:20,21,* his primary concern is to understand why his relationship with God has gone astray.

> *If I sin, what do I do to you, you watcher of*
> *mankind? Why have you made me your mark?*
> *Why have I become a burden to you?*
> *Why do you not pardon my transgression and*
> *take away my iniquity? For now I shall lie in the*
> *earth; you will seek me, but I shall not be.*

Zophar, alas, doesn't attempt to understand Job's questioning, and he has no patience with Job or comfort for his outbursts of pain and distress. Zophar is a relentlessly judgemental man who thinks Job is actually getting less than he deserves. Instead, he goes right for the jugular in *Job 11:4-6:*

> *"For you say, 'My doctrine is pure, and*
> *I am clean in God's eyes.'*
> *But oh, that God would speak and open his lips to you,*
> *and that he would tell you the secrets of wisdom!*
> *For he is manifold in understanding. Know then that*
> *God exacts of you less than your guilt deserves."*

Zophar's problem is that he comes to Job's situation convinced he knows that God believes Job has sinned, and that this is the root cause of Job's problem. He thinks that things could have been, indeed should have been a lot worse for Job because God has actually overlooked some of Job's wrongdoing. Talk about pouring water on a drowning man; with friends like Zophar, who needs enemies?

Nor does our learned friend improve. In **Job 11:7&11** Zophar proceeds to explain, in rather grand language, what Job already knew, namely that God knows all, sees all, and is certainly aware of all of Job's wrongdoings.

> *"Can you find out the deep things of God? Can*
> *you find out the limit of the Almighty?*
> *For he knows worthless men; when he sees*
> *iniquity, will he not consider it?"*

And it gets worse, because in **Job 11:12** he goes on to imply that Job is like an unteachable donkey. Somehow I don't think I'd want Zophar either as a grief counsellor or a diplomat!

Having now assumed he knows that Job's condition is all the result of stubbornly unacknowledged wickedness, he goes on to explain in **Job 11:14&17** that if Job repents and turns away from his sins, God will bless him and give him a life of happiness and security.

> *If iniquity is in your hand, put it far away, and*
> *let not injustice dwell in your tents.*
> *And your life will be brighter than the noonday;*
> *its darkness will be like the morning.*

This man should have been in telemarketing! He'd clearly promise anything to anyone just to win an argument.

That said, in one sense Zophar's claim is actually right, at least in principle. It's absolutely true that a secure life of faith and contentment is always based on penitent obedience to God. However, Zophar's pious and entirely theoretical response was completely inappropriate in this situation on two counts.

Firstly, he was wrong in assuming that Job had brought all his troubles upon himself by his own sin, because we are told by God at the outset that Job was a blameless man. Secondly, Zophar was wrong in assuming that by admitting to his sins and being obedient to God, Job would then automatically have an idyllic life.

It is a sad fact that some otherwise well meaning Christians get deluded into believing, often unconsciously, that God automatically rewards our attempts to lead a good and blameless life. If only it were that simple! The reality is that more than a few Christians end up leading lives which are pretty tough and demanding, in some cases even dying for their faith. Martin Luther King and Dietrich Bonhoeffer are two modern examples that come to mind; King was shot at a street rally in the USA, and Bonhoeffer was hanged in Nazi Germany. Both men were just 39 years old. Gospel ministry has always had its risks. Look no further than **Acts 7,** where right at the very beginning of the Christian church we find Stephen being stoned to death, simply for preaching the Gospel. To this day there are all too many countries where Christians are imprisoned and even executed for their faith. Just Google Christian persecution if you want to read more on this.

But back to Job. Unsurprisingly, he was very unimpressed by all the presumptuous and theoretical advice being provided. So in **Job 13:1,4&5** he offers these friends a very blunt response:

> *"what you know, I also know."*

and goes on to tell them:

> *"As for you, you whitewash with lies;*
> *worthless physicians are you all.*

Oh that you would keep silent,
and it would be your wisdom!"

In this rather frank exchange of views, his friends are simply told that he doesn't value their advice, and they should just shut up! Despite its blunt style, this passage contains several important lessons for us too.

The first lesson is that we cannot demand "logical" human explanations based on cause and effect for everything we experience. We often instinctively proceed down this path, because that's how western reductionist intellectual inquiry often works. Tempting though it is, we shouldn't try to limit God in this way. Right at the very end of the book God admonishes Job's three friends sternly for effectively trying to do exactly this in *Job 42:7*. Speaking directly to Eliphaz, God says:

My anger burns against you and against your two friends, for you have not spoken of me what is right, as my servant Job has.

It is a dangerous path to tread, one often unhelpful to us or others in distress, just to assume that whatever is happening is driven by a simple human model of cause and effect. We cannot acknowledge God as infinitely wise and powerful on the one hand, and then on the other demand simple, finite, and sometimes ill-informed human explanations for everything that happens. Job's friends are rightly admonished for misrepresenting God's relationship with Job. So, especially if we are counselling others, we should be very wary of offering them simplistic explanations about whatever is concerning them. We must take care not to misrepresent or oversimplify the nature of the relationship between God and ourselves as believers just in the interests of providing what may turn out to be rather facile spiritual comfort,

The second lesson is that we should never assume suffering must be God punishing us for some specific action. God does not work this way, and like it or not, human suffering is, was, and always will be, inherent to living in our present fallen world. We should never forget that. **Genesis 3** describes events causing the perfection of God's creation to be shattered by the disobedience of Adam and Eve in the Garden of Eden. From then on mankind has lived in a broken world, one which the Bible tells us will always be marked by pain, by a hostile nature, and by human corruption. It is only with Christ's final return that we will receive deliverance from the many hazards we will continue to encounter in this fallen world, as Paul explains in **Romans 8:21:**

> *...the creation itself will be set free from its*
> *bondage to corruption and obtain the freedom*
> *of the glory of the children of God.*

This also refers to the new heaven and new earth described in **Rev 21:4.**

Jesus talked about this same glorious future Himself when his disciples asked Him about the end of the age and His return in **Matt 24**. There He explained to them to expect wars, famines, earthquakes, persecution and death before that day. Paul likewise reminds us in **Romans 8:18** that we have to expect suffering, and that we always need to maintain the long view, confident in our eternal hope.

> *For I consider that the sufferings of this*
> *present time are not worth comparing with*
> *the glory that is to be revealed to us.*

James 5:10 reminds us that throughout salvation history suffering has always been one of the costs of faith.

> *As an example of suffering and patience, brothers,*
> *take the prophets who spoke in the name of the Lord.*

The same reminder is echoed in *1Peter 4:13* telling us that suffering is part of the Christian journey.

> *But rejoice insofar as you share Christ's*
> *sufferings, that you may also rejoice and*
> *be glad when his glory is revealed.*

As we can see, the Bible makes it quite clear that the possibility of suffering for a life of faith and witness as the cost of discipleship has always been there. Not a punishment, but rather as a cost that ever so faintly reflects the unimaginable cost of Jesus going to the cross for you and for me. The history of Christian missions in the 20th century alone gives us many examples of this. Talk to a Christian brother or sister from one of the fifty countries currently identified as being hostile to the Gospel, especially in the third world. They'll tell you about suffering for their faith, not about being punished for sin.

The foregoing discussion doesn't mean that God never sends punishment and suffering as a response to sinful behaviour. The Assyrian and Babylonian invasions of the Israelites, and the exile in Babylon were very much a consequence of centuries of national disobedience. Nor should we ever discount the fact that God sometimes allows suffering to teach us lessons. Paul explains this in *Romans 5:3-5 :*

More than that, we rejoice in our sufferings,
knowing that suffering produces endurance,
and endurance produces character,
and character produces hope,
and hope does not put us to shame, because God's
love has been poured into our hearts through
the Holy Spirit who has been given to us.

Given what the Bible tells us about suffering, as we try to fathom the reasons for Job's troubles, unlike Eliphaz, Bildad, Zophar and Elihu, we should avoid being tempted into simple cause and effect explanations of why we suffer.

Therefore the third lesson we should take from Job and his friends is that it just isn't true that faith and obedience will automatically lead to a peaceful and idyllic life. As we've seen earlier in this chapter, being a Christian is sometimes a risky business, and none of us can escape the possibility that we may, for whatever reason, be exposed to suffering. I think, therefore, we need to be a little wary of churches that preach a "prosperity gospel". It is absolutely wrong to encourage anyone into accepting Jesus as their Saviour on a promise that their newfound faith will automatically lead them to an earthly life without problems or challenges or will automatically solve all their personal or financial difficulties.

Yes, the Bible certainly says that God will bless us richly if we lead a life of faith. This is absolutely true spiritually, but it may not necessarily mean material blessing. ***Psalm 1:1*** certainly says:

Blessed is the man who walks not in the counsel of the wicked nor stands in the way of sinners, nor sits in the seat of scoffers.

And it goes on to say

in all that he does he prospers.

But in ***2Tim 2:3*** we get the flip side of this, as Paul gives his protege important and realistic advice, reminding him not to expect his life of service to be easy:

Share in suffering as a good soldier of Christ Jesus.

Of his own hardships he goes on in ***2Tim 4:18*** to declare that whatever happens he is confident in God's eternal provision:

***The Lord will rescue me from every
evil deed and bring me safely
into His heavenly kingdom.***

I have a friend, a faithful Christian man all his life, who has lived through an experience that has some real parallels with Job's story. For many years, he was happily married, had a great family, and was doing a job he loved. Then his wife died prematurely after a long battle with cancer, and around the same time the job he loved came to an unexpected end. Despite this tragedy, I have a vivid memory of speaking with him just after his wife passed away, and when I'd said all the usual things, he simply said to me *"John, I understand that God is no man's debtor"*.

I know he still misses his wife every day. Yet I am also certain that even though his grief remains very real, from within his mature Christian faith he knows he won't get any real explanations about what he's been through this side of heaven. Until then, he won't know exactly why his life was suddenly turned upside down. But I do know he's certain his wife is now with her Lord, and I do know he's content with that because he is confident she is in the hands of an infinitely wise and loving God. Whatever his immediate situation and the inexplicable pain it has caused him, his life continues as an excellent example of someone who has come to understand better than most of us what being on God's time really means. Very importantly, he has not been destroying himself by looking for unobtainable explanations, nor is he burning with resentment about what might have been. His energy and focus has been redirected to supporting his extended family, and to using his professional skills and experience in productive Christian service.

If there is one important thing to learn from Job's saga and from others who have experienced unexplained suffering, it is this: we really are always on God's time. He is not our debtor, we are in his hands, and we must always put our trust in His purposes. Yes, we may well experience suffering along the way for a variety of often complex and sometimes inexplicable reasons. That has certainly been my experience, and probably yours too. I know I won't get answers in this life for some of the things I have experienced, although I have to say that in some cases in experiencing trials God has shown me that what seemed unpleasant at the time was ultimately for my own good. I also know, in my many years as a Christian, that God has blessed me in ways that have exceeded anything I could have ever imagined, much less deserved, and I am deeply thankful to Him every day for this.

Job finally accepted his situation when God spoke to him in *Job 40*. After all his struggles, his real fear still remained that God was angry with him, and he did not understand why he had been so harshly treated, nor that he had sinned. Yet for all that, his confidence in God never wavered. One of my favourite verses is found in Job's reply to the rather tedious Zophar. Speaking of God he says in *Job 13:15 :*

"Though he slay me, I will hope in Him ."

I cannot imagine a more complete expression of trust in God's purposes for any of us than this. Job's final relief came when he acknowledged God's infinite power, wisdom and perfect justice, when he acknowledged that he had no right to expect an explanation for any of the events that had overtaken him, let alone expect to understand them. So he confesses to God in *Job 42:3:*

> *"Who is this that hides counsel without knowledge?*
> *Therefore I have uttered what I did not understand,*
> *things too wonderful for me, which I did not know."*

What shines through as we come to the end of Job's story is his persevering trust in God and His purposes throughout all his trials, despite the misguided arguments of his friends. God is rightly pleased that His confidence in Job's trust has been vindicated. Job's only real fear, as I remarked earlier, that for some reason he might have lost God's favour, was finally allayed and His relationship with God which was of such central importance to him was restored along with his household. Contrast this with Job's friends whose assumption from the outset was that Job had done something deserving God's condemnation and punishment, and that he should confess and repent of his misdeeds. Happily Job was not taken in by their unfounded assumptions and steadfastly maintained his own innocence as well as his trust in God. Job's perseverance and his vindication are a great lesson for us all.

I want to conclude this chapter with a reminder that just as Job steadfastly trusted in God's purposes, and persevered in his trust through all his trials despite the misleading advice of his friends, so God tells us that whatever challenges we may face in our earthly life, we always have His promise of salvation. He promises that we will be in His presence for eternity if we truly repent of our many shortcomings, if we genuinely believe that by His death and resurrection Jesus has paid the penalty for our sin once and for all time, and so by His sacrifice we are made perfect in God's sight. That is God's guarantee, that is His eternal promise, and His promise never wavers. As Paul tells us in **Rom 8:38,39:**

> *For I am sure that neither death nor life, nor angels nor*
> *rulers, nor things present nor things to come, nor powers,*
> *nor height nor depth, nor anything else in all*
> *creation, will be able to separate us from the*
> *love of God in Christ Jesus our Lord.*

In any situation, as Job discovered, we are inescapably on God's time. We serve His purposes whether they be hard or easy at any given moment. If we have claimed God's amazing promises of salvation, then, like Job, we truly can hope in Him alone.

Chapter 7
PRAYER

The story is told of a little boy kneeling beside his bed with his mother and grandma quietly saying his prayers.

"Dear God, please bless Mummy and Daddy, my baby sister, and Grandma, and please don't give me any scary dreams." Then without any warning, looking up and shouting, "And please God, don't forget to give me a bike for my birthday!"

"There is no need to shout," said his mother. "God isn't deaf."

"I know," said the little boy, "but Grandma is."

Let's talk about prayer, but hopefully with a little less self-interest than the small boy in our story. Prayer is a really big subject, one website lists over 200 books about it, but here I just want to focus on what we can learn from St Paul, because his life and letters recorded in the New Testament demonstrate just how much his amazing ministry was based on prayer. So just what is prayer and what is its purpose? Is it just about asking God to do this, or to give us that? And are we always the ones who initiate prayer? Just how we answer these and other questions about prayer will rather depend on whether we look at prayer from our perspective or from God's perspective. I guess we've all had requests, or perhaps some urgent need, that we truly believe to be within God's best intentions for us, and then asked Him to get on with making it happen. And it's tempting to think that maybe God won't act until we pray and give Him a nudge about it, often with a sometimes unconscious view that the outcome of our prayer is more about our needs than about the sovereign will of God.

I want to suggest to you at the outset that if we have a view of prayer which fails to put the sovereignty of God first, or in one way or another fails to acknowledge that God is the sovereign Lord of the Universe, we risk being in a biblically and theologically untenable position and unable to really understand prayer and its purpose. The clear message of the whole of the Bible is that God is in ultimate control of all things across all of salvation history. And here I'm not just thinking about big picture stuff; God's sovereignty and His plan of salvation for all mankind extend into the very detail of all of our lives. Matthew 10 and Luke 12 both record Jesus reminding His Disciples:

"The very hairs of your head are all numbered".

God intends all of our lives to be lived according to His will, according to His plan and His purpose, and certainly not just according to our own desires, no matter how well intentioned they might be. Paul explains this very clearly in his letters to the churches at Philippi and Ephesus.

Philippians 2:12, 13
Therefore, my beloved, as you have always obeyed,
so now, not only as in my presence but much more
in my absence, work out your own salvation with

fear and trembling, for it is God who works in you,
both to will and to work for his good pleasure.

Ephesians 2: 6-10
and (God) raised us up with him and seated us with
Him in the heavenly places in Christ Jesus,
so that in the coming ages He might show the immeasurable
riches of His grace in kindness toward us in Christ Jesus.
For by grace you have been saved through faith. And
this is not your own doing; it is the gift of God, not a
result of works, so that no one may boast. For we are His
workmanship, created in Christ Jesus for good works, which
God prepared beforehand, that we should walk in them.

Paul makes it absolutely clear that every believer must aim to live within God's sovereign will, and so be an active and obedient part of the outworking of His complete plan of salvation. This plan aims to bring glory to God alone, and this plan has been made complete and perfect once and for all time in the cross of Christ. We need to recognise that we are just one small part of a plan that spans all of human history and beyond into eternity. And if we believe and embrace that truth, we cannot treat prayer as a means of just stirring up God to get on with the things which are of immediate concern to us.

In fact, the reality is quite the opposite. First and foremost, as the previous passage from **Ephesians** reminds us, God intends us to live lives that are aligned to His will, aligned to His plan and purpose for us. So prayer cannot just be a personal shopping list. If we believe God is sovereign, if we believe that He has revealed Himself to the world and redeemed us through sending His Son Jesus to die for our sins, then ultimately, only His will and purposes matter. Our priority in prayer must be to focus on being part of that plan, and so when we ask things of God it must be because they are part of it too. Graeme Goldsworthy writing about prayer defines it as "our response to God as He speaks to us". This then, is prayer seen from God's perspective.

The Lord's prayer, which Jesus gave to His Disciples, and to us, as a model for our own prayers makes His expected priorities in our prayer life abundantly clear as He taught His disciples how to pray in *Matthew 6:9&10 (& Luke 11).*

> *Pray then like this:"Our Father in heaven,hallowed*
> *be your name. Your kingdom come,*
> *your will be done, on earth as it is in heaven.*

The very first thing we see is Jesus' acknowledgement of God the Father and His pre-eminence, and then Jesus goes on to pray for the final fulfillment of salvation history with His own return to rule over all creation. We get the first hint of this when Jesus begins His public ministry by announcing in *Mark 1:14 &15:*

> *The time is fulfilled, and the kingdom of God is*
> *at hand; repent and believe in the gospel.*

This is a very far cry from starting prayer with a shopping list of things that happen to be concerning as at some given moment in time. This is the prayer of someone whose priorities and concerns are first and foremost eternal.

Many of you will remember the devastation of New Orleans in the US by hurricane Katrina in 2005. Then a second hurricane, Rita, appeared and was set to do even more damage. Many people prayed that this wouldn't happen, and indeed Rita weakened and then diverted away from New Orleans. This truly was answered prayer. But did it mean that the prayers of many Christians caused God to make a hasty last minute adjustment to the micro-climatology of the US east coast weather system? No, it meant that God had allowed many Christians to participate in the exercise of what would always have been His sovereign will. This is a very different take on events compared with treating prayer as just asking God to be our local trouble shooter.

If we see prayer from this "God first" biblical perspective, then as Christians we should never ever feel we are unworthy or inadequate to pray, or that we cannot come before God's throne of grace because of our failures and the sins we commit which are the reality of every Christian's daily struggle with our fallen natures. We should never be ashamed if our prayers seem less eloquent than others (I've heard some Oscar winning performances in prayer meetings!) We are redeemed by the death and resurrection of the Lord Jesus, and God promises in scripture that nothing can ever take that away from us. This means that whatever our failings, whatever our personal emotions at the time, whatever our verbal skills when we do pray, we have the promise in God's Word that we can always come to God in prayer, and that when we come, we do so on equal terms with every other Christian on the planet, past, and future. Because this is not about us, it is about Jesus who has redeemed us and changed our relationship with God once and for all time and when we pray it is He who intercedes with the Father for us as John has explained in *1John 2:1,2:*

> *...if anyone does sin, we have an advocate*
> *with the Father, Jesus Christ the righteous. He*
> *is the propitiation for our sins, and not for ours*
> *only but also for the sins of the whole world.*

We must never forget that the reason we can have a relationship with God at all is because God made us in His image. We are a unique part of His creation with unique responsibilities. God has given us the gift of thought, reasoning, and language. Indeed, the whole of creation came into being because God <u>spoke</u>, and said let there be...light, night and day, water and land, plants and animals and so on, and finally, He created man in His own image. God has used His gift of language both in revealing Himself to us and in allowing us to respond to Him.

There is a great example of prayer in the Godhead itself as Jesus prays to His Father in the Garden of Gethsemane, knowing as he prays just what He would endure on the Cross. Understandably, His human response is to ask for relief from the horrendous agony to come. Yet we see in **Mark 14:35 &36** that even Jesus, in this most extraordinary of human struggles, submits His prayer to the sovereign will of His Father.

And going a little farther, he fell on the ground and prayed that, if it were possible, the hour might pass from him. And he said, "Abba, Father, all things are possible for you. Remove this cup from me. Yet not what I will, but what you will.

That is surely <u>the</u> benchmark example in all of salvation history of prayer being aligned to the sovereign will of God.

One of the joys and indeed the miracles of being a Christian is the presence of the Holy Spirit within us. He is the one who sustains our faith, and He is the one who makes praying a practical reality for us. In **Romans 8:26,27** and **Ephesians 6:18** for example, Paul urges us all to use this great gift, and use it well.

Likewise the Spirit helps us in our weakness. For we do not know what to pray for as we ought, but the Spirit himself intercedes for us with groanings too deep for words. And he who searches hearts knows what is the mind of the Spirit, because the Spirit intercedes for the saints according to the will of God.

...praying at all times in the Spirit, with all prayer and supplication. To that end keep alert with all perseverance, making supplication for all the saints.

If we are ever tempted to take prayer for granted, it is worthwhile remembering the reasons we can pray at all, and what a great privilege God has given us in the gift of prayer. In summary, we can pray because:

- We are made in God's image
- We are made righteous before God in Christ who intercedes for us with the Father
- We have the Holy Spirit within us

Even so, you might still be tempted to think; "if God has everything in hand, do we really need to pray at all?" But on the contrary, God wants us to pray, and He wants us to pray constantly so that we will continue to live within His sovereign will. John Calvin has some very practical advice for us when we pray.

"Our prayer must not be self-centred. It must arise not only because we feel our own need as a burden we must lay upon God, but also because we are so bound up in love for our fellow men that we feel their need as acutely as our own. To make intercession for men is the most powerful and practical way in which we can express our love for them."

If we need further encouragement about the value of prayer, remember the Bible also makes it plain that when we pray through the power of the Holy Spirit and in the great name of Jesus, our prayer will always be heard and always be answered as Jesus Himself assures us in *Matthew 21:22* and *John 14:13&14:*

> *And whatever you ask in prayer, you*
> *will receive, if you have faith.*

> *Whatever you ask in my name, this I will do, that*
> *the Father may be glorified in the Son. If you*
> *ask me anything in my name, I will do it.*

But this doesn't mean that God just gives us a blank cheque when we pray. Nor when you and I pray in the great name of Jesus, are we just using a password. No, we are acknowledging that we can speak to God only because the shed blood of Jesus has put us in a right relationship with Him. We are acknowledging that we are participants in God's grand plan of salvation in which the Cross has provided the final, permanent victory over sin and death. In short, we pray wanting to be part of God's sovereign will within His great plan of salvation.

1John 5:14&15 summarises this really well:

> *And this is the confidence that we have toward him, that*
> *if we ask anything according to his will he hears us. And*
> *if we know that he hears us in whatever we ask, we know*
> *that we have the requests that we have asked of him.*

Scripture is crystal clear, faithful prayer is always answered, but it is never for us to dictate what that answer will, or should, be.

Let me return for a moment to the issue of how prayer is answered, starting with Jesus in the Garden of Gethsemane. Three times He asked to be relieved of the Cross, but praise God that even so Jesus submitted himself to God's greater will. When Paul prayed that his "thorn in the flesh", which was probably some chronic medical problem, to be removed God said no. And why? So that Christ would be glorified, not Paul, and to keep him from becoming proud. David prayed for his dying child who had been conceived in quite sinful circumstances, but God denied him healing. Jonah and Elijah both had similar experiences. The outcome of prayer is always subject to God's will. It is a real testament to our faith when no matter what we might want to occur, we acknowledge that only God in His sovereignty ultimately knows what is in our best interest.

And a brief word about who we pray to. The normal biblical pattern is that we pray to the Father in the name of Jesus, by the power of the Spirit. We can pray specifically to any member of the Godhead, but we do risk confusing the distinctive roles of the three persons of the Trinity. There seem to be only three examples of directly addressing Jesus in the NT; Stephen responding to his vision of Jesus in *Acts 7*, Paul responding to the voice of Jesus on the road to Damascus in *Acts 9*, and John responding to Jesus in *Revelation 22*.

So what sort of things should we be praying about? *1 Thessalonians 2&3*, and passages like it, give us a powerful example from Paul to follow. Paul visited Thessalonica on his second missionary journey, but only stayed about three weeks before hostility from local Jews forced him to leave, and they then persecuted the new converts as well. Greeks there who were already converts to Judaism, found an attraction to a Gospel in which they weren't seen as second class citizens, and the Jews hated this. Paul had a great love and concern for the new church in

Thessalonica as his letters to them show. He was desperate to know how they were getting on, desperate to get back to give them more in-depth teaching about the Gospel, and desperate to refute his critics there who reviled him, and then when they had made life there impossible for him, accused him of running away. Conversely though, he was also absolutely delighted to learn from Timothy how well these new Christians were doing.

In every way, Paul's letters to this and other new testament churches reflect his overwhelming concern for their personal and spiritual welfare as an integral part of his overall passion for the advancement of the Kingdom of God. Paul's great love and care for the people in the fledgling churches he had either founded, or ministered to and encouraged, totally pervades the New Testament. Time and again in his letters he begins by saying how much he thanks God for his fellow believers, and for what God has done in their lives. Don Carson identifies 42 separate passages in Paul's writings where he is either praying or talking about prayer for the churches and the people he has ministered to in his missionary odyssey. This surely, is firm evidence for the power and place prayer should have in every Christian's spiritual journey.

Perhaps nowhere more than in *1Thessalonians 2&3* do we see the passionate outpouring of Paul's love and care for the people of God, something which characterises his whole ministry. In *1Thessalonians 2:17&18* , Paul explains how much he wanted to come and visit them, but was prevented from doing so by Satan for reasons unknown (although some have speculated that it may have involved some sort of personal illness). Then in *verses 19&20* he asks and answers this question:

For what is our hope or joy or crown of boasting
before our Lord Jesus at his coming? Is it not
you? For you are our glory and joy.

Paul's twofold delight and joy is firstly that they are now believers, and secondly that in the eternal future he will be able to rejoice with them in the presence of the Lord Jesus. This is not about Paul or his endeavours, it is about the joy he feels in knowing what God has done in Jesus for these people. He goes on to explain his intense frustration in being unable to travel there in *1 Thessalonians 5:1-5:*

Therefore when we could bear it no longer, we were willing
to be left behind at Athens alone, and we sent Timothy,
our brother and God's coworker in the gospel of Christ,
to establish and exhort you in your faith, that no one be
moved by these afflictions. For you yourselves know that
we are destined for this. For when we were with you,
we kept telling you beforehand that we were to suffer
affliction, just as it has come to pass, and just as you know.
For this reason, when I could bear it no longer, I sent to
learn about your faith, for fear that somehow the tempter
had tempted you and our labour would be in vain.

Timothy's good news of their faith and love was a huge personal encouragement to Paul, and in God's providence it came at a time when he was feeling pretty downcast and needed the Lord's encouragement. Therefore we should not be surprised that his immediate response was to think about how to pray in response to such great news as he explains in *1 Thessalonians 3:8-10.* What a great lesson this is to us all in the good use of prayer.

For now we really live, since you are standing firm in the Lord. How can we thank God enough for you in return for all the joy we have in the presence of our God because of you? Night and day we pray most earnestly that we may see you again and supply what is lacking in your faith.

One of the hallmarks of Paul's ministry, and not least in his prayer life, is his utter selflessness. His first reaction is to say what a new lease of life Timothy's good news about the Thessalonians has given him. but not for personal reasons because he immediately goes on to ask how when he prays, can he thank God enough for the work He has done in nurturing the spiritual growth of these people. Then Paul tells them that he is praying he can come back to nurture their newfound faith further. This is all about Paul being a servant of God's grace, being part of His sovereign will, and about the joy of the work of bringing unbelievers into the Kingdom of God. What a great example for us all to follow, and he ends this part of his letter with this spontaneous prayer for these Christians in *1 Thessalonians 3:11-13:*

Now may our God and Father himself, and our Lord Jesus, direct our way to you, and may the Lord make you increase and abound in love for one another and for all, as we do for you, so that he may establish your hearts blameless in holiness before our God and Father, at the coming of our Lord Jesus with all his saints.

Paul makes three specific requests in this prayer, and these too are an important part of the example he sets for us in his prayer life.

His first request is that God might make it possible for him to visit them. We know that God did answer Paul's prayer on his third missionary journey when he visited Macedonia as **Acts 20** tells us and so was able to be a great encouragement to Christians in that region. The lesson for us is that like Paul, we too should always see the advancement of the Kingdom of God and the spiritual welfare of fellow believers as a constant priority in our prayer and service.

His second request is that Jesus will increase their love towards each other, just as he Paul loves them, and that they should also love all those in their community. In this way they will then be living witnesses to the transforming power of the Gospel and reflect the love that God has shown for his creation in sending Jesus to redeem us. So we too, individually, and as a church, should make our witness to God's love amongst us and to the wider community a prayer priority.

His third request is that God will strengthen and sustain these Christians, and continue His work of holiness (sanctification) within each of them so they will be prepared when Jesus returns. The new testament church had a very immediate sense about the second coming which I think with the passage of time we have in varying degrees lost. So another lesson from Paul's prayer is our need to pray for the spiritual lives of our fellow Christians, and mindful of Jesus's parable of the wise and foolish virgins in **Matthew 25**, pray constantly that we will be prepared to meet the Lord when He returns. Paul has so much to teach us about maintaining a faithful and expectant prayer life.

Let me now go back to where I began. I said that prayer is fundamentally about seeking to be obedient participants in God's sovereign plan for His creation within salvation history. That plan centres on the Cross in which God has fulfilled His promise to redeem us from sin and death. God wills that everyone should be saved, and in being saved that we should be progressively transformed to be like Jesus, and ultimately be ready to face Him on the day of judgement. This is what Paul prays for, and rejoices about, throughout all of his writings, and this should be the foundation of our prayer life as well.

This mustn't stop us from praying about the specific and immediate needs of others or ourselves, as long as we always understand that we do so as active participants in serving God's sovereign will and purposes. We cannot ever just treat God as the local Mr Fix-it in our prayer life.

Let me conclude by suggesting five prayer priorities which we might usefully learn from the life and witness of the apostle Paul.

Firstly, we should always be thankful to God for His wonderful gift of prayer which we enjoy because we are made in His image.

Secondly, our prayer should always reflect our desire to live within God's sovereign will.

Thirdly, we should thank God and pray for the spread of the Gospel, and for the spiritual and physical welfare of all our fellow Christians, and especially new believers.

Fourthly, we should pray that our love for our fellow believers and for those around us in the community will increase our witness to God's love and transforming grace at work within us.

Fifthly, we should pray that individually, and as a church, we will always be spiritually prepared for the return of Jesus.

Let me finish with a salutary quote from John Calvin who, speaking about prayer observed that:

> *Believers do not pray with the view of informing God about things unknown to Him, or of exciting Him to do His duty, or of urging Him as though He were reluctant. On the contrary, they pray in order that they may arouse themselves to seek Him, and that they may*

*declare that from Him alone they hope and expect, both
for themselves and for others, all good things.*

In other words, we must always pray with confident trust that God will always provide for us in ways that are ultimately in our very best interest.

Chapter 8

TEMPTATION

Some readers, especially anyone who has worked in the finance industry, will be familiar with the story of Bernie Madoff, probably the most famous fraudster in modern history. He started out as a well respected New York investment broker, and at one time was the chairman of Nasdaq, the world's first global electronic exchange for trading shares. Despite his apparently impressive financial pedigree, all was not quite as it seemed with Madoff, and in 2009 he was convicted of running the biggest Ponzi scheme in history: named after Charles Ponzi who popularised this particular scam in the 1920s. The idea is pretty simple: you offer prospective investors vastly better returns on the money they want to invest than they can get in the regular market, and then use their own supposedly invested money to pay the big dividends you promised them. The snag is of course, that you can only keep this up for as long as you can continue getting money from other new and similarly gullible investors. Most Ponzi frauds collapse fairly quickly when the scheme runs out of new investors, or when too many people want to withdraw their money from the scheme at once. Ultimately, it is a bit like trying to pull yourself up by your own boot laces.

Madoff's scam was unusual because, unlike most Ponzi frauds, it ran undiscovered for decades! The whole scheme was so complex that it still remains an open question as to whether the size of the final fraud has really been fully determined. What we do know for certain is that investors lost tens of billions of dollars and there were no happy endings. Lives were ruined, Madoff himself was jailed for life, dying there in 2021, and tragically, one of his sons committed suicide while another died of cancer. Ponzi frauds are a very good example of something that seems too good to be true being exactly that!

One of the downsides of our internet age, is that it has become a lot easier to run dishonest scams like this and to operate them internationally when attempting to persuade potential investors to part with their hard earned goods and money. Phishing is another of the more prevalent scams in the internet age, and one that loses people hundreds and hundreds of millions of dollars every year. Victims are sent messages from supposedly reputable sources, usually aimed either at tricking them into revealing passwords, bank details etc., or luring them into investing in bogus schemes promising huge returns.

The basic driver for most scams is greed in which fraudsters use deception in one form or another to try and take from others what is not rightfully theirs, and doing whatever it takes to get it. This very often amounts to good old fashioned theft driven by coveting and it almost always has unhappy consequences. It should never be confused with making legitimate profits from business activities involving the trading of bona fide goods and services which is another matter entirely. The 10th and last commandment specifically warns us against coveting, and not least because it too easily has a domino effect leading to all kinds of other sinful behaviour, even amongst otherwise apparently respectable people.

For a textbook example of covetousness and the domino effect it can create, look no further than the infamous but well known story of David and Bathsheba recorded in **2Samuel 11 &12**. King David takes a stroll on the roof of the palace after his afternoon snooze, and sees below a stunningly beautiful woman who sets his royal pulse racing. He learns quickly she is Bathsheba, the wife of a court official named Uriah who was away at a war with the Ammonites in one of those seemingly endless disputes over middle eastern real estate; so the appearance of her husband wasn't an immediate problem. David has Bathsheba brought to the palace, makes her an improper royal offer she can't refuse, and in an age of decidedly unsafe sex, she becomes pregnant.

Things go downhill pretty rapidly from there. David soon realises he is now socially and morally compromised, and sets about covering his tracks. He calls Uriah back from the war and encourages him to enjoy some home comforts. But in this he has a notable lack of success, because, unfortunately for David, Uriah is a rather proper man who feels it would be inappropriate, even wrong, to start enjoying domestic life while his fellow countrymen involved in the current battle are away and engaged in a major military operation. Even after liquor and bribes, David fails to get his loyal subject to go home and sleep with his wife. This tawdry scheme was of course designed to try and make Bathsheba's expected child appear to be Uriah's. It's all a bit like a B grade TV soapie, but without the risk of a modern day paternity test!

When his dishonest plan fails, David proceeds with plan B which is much nastier. He arranges for Uriah to go back to the most dangerous battle front in the Ammonite war where hopefully he will get killed and so solve David's problem permanently. This dreadful scheme succeeds, and Uriah dies as planned. David then marries Bathsheba, but the child she bore him dies. David's covetousness has brought him nothing but tragedy and disrepute, until he finally recognises what a truly dreadful thing he has done. His deeply moving words of repentance for his sinful behaviour are recorded in *Psalm 51:1&2:*

> *Have mercy on me, O God, according to your steadfast love;*
> *according to your abundant mercy blot out my transgressions.*
> *Wash me thoroughly from my iniquity,*
> *and cleanse me from my sin!*

And then further in verse 17 we go on to see his repentant sinner's confidence in God's grace and mercy:

> *The sacrifices of God are a broken spirit; a broken*
> *and contrite heart, O God, you will not despise.*

David's story is a notable example of coveting, and provides a graphic illustration of the way breaking one of God's laws can have a domino effect leading to more and more sinful consequences. Happily, when he realises the enormity of what he has done, we also see David's confidence in God's grace and mercy; the same confidence available to every Christian believer when we fail to meet God's standard of holiness.

As Christians, we live under two sets of laws. There are the laws of the state such as those which set strict limits on how fast you can drive your car, laws forbidding you from selling miracle medicines that guarantee to cure diseases like cancer, and so on. In attempting to protect us, our civil laws are often quite complex, occasionally contradictory, sometimes border on the incomprehensible and often involve mountains of documentation...as any successful lawyer will happily tell you.

Then there is God's Law, the 10 commandments, so concise they are easily written on a single A4 page. They are His blueprint for living, His yardstick of righteousness, and the standard by which our behaviour as Christians is measured. These laws, although simple, present us in a systemic sense with an unsurpassed model of moral perfection. They are self-consistent and cover every essential aspect of human behaviour. And although they are often diluted, and sometimes even flatly denied by modern secular critics, they remain the essential moral and ethical foundation of the society we enjoy today. Like Bernie Madoff and others, David's troubles all started by breaking the 10th and last commandment which warns us against trying to possess things we don't own or have the right to use.

In this chapter I want to explore two related issues about coveting: why it is so dangerous, and what the law against coveting itself reveals about the overall perfection of God's law and about His expectations for Christian life and conduct.

Firstly let's remind ourselves what the 10th commandment actually says in *Exodus 20:17:*

> *You shall not covet your neighbour's house. You shall not covet your neighbour's wife, or his male servant or his female servant, his ox or his donkey, or anything that is your neighbour's.*

At first glance you might find this to be an amusingly dated list of covetable items, and at one level you'd be right. But lay that small distraction aside for a moment and let's analyse David's situation in a bit more detail. He starts by breaking the 10th commandment in wanting a relationship with a woman actually married to somebody else. Then he breaks the 8th commandment in abducting Bathsheba. By the social standards of the day this was really an act of theft. That was quickly followed by breaking the 7th commandment in having an illicit sexual relationship with a woman married to someone else; all of which ended up in Bathsheba's pregnancy. Then if that wasn't enough, he breaks both the 9th commandment about lying, and the 6th commandment about murder by engineering the death of Bathsheba's unfortunate husband to make his covetous actions appear legitimate. It's a pretty ugly story that ends with David enmeshed in a litany of sinful acts.

David's initial covetousness, while bad enough in itself, had led him into an avalanche of sinful behaviour ultimately resulting in the death of a decent innocent man. This is the domino effect writ large. But pause a moment as we think about this. We aren't talking here about some nasty Old Testament villain (no shortage of them in *Judges* alone), this is David! This is God's anointed King, this is the man described as being after God's own heart, the man God chose to bring Israel into its brief golden age, the man who plays a key role in the unfolding of salvation history culminating in the coming of Jesus as the promised Messiah, the one who, as prophesied, was David's direct descendant.

It is a graphic reminder that even apparent spiritual giants can become victim to their fallen natures. Not a single one of us is immune, and as history shows, those called by God to Christian leadership need to remain especially vigilant in their daily walk with the Lord. The 20th and 21st century church alone has far too many examples of leaders who have been guilty of misconduct involving everything from the abuse of vulnerable children to financial malfeasance. We must constantly remind ourselves that we are all vulnerable to temptations of every kind. Paul rightly warns us in *Romans 3:23:*

> *all have sinned and fall short of the glory of God.*

Coveting is a time-bomb just waiting to create immense collateral damage even amongst the most committed Christian believers.

Some three thousand years after David, we need to remind ourselves that coveting and its consequences have not changed, because our basic fallen human nature has not changed. One modern writer has summarised the main motives for murder as being lust, love, loathing and loot, which pretty well covers the most common causes of coveting and its consequences. Sure, we can be thankful it doesn't necessarily lead to murder, but all too commonly it involves misplaced sexual desire, the destruction of relationships, or deceptive attempts to acquire money or assets not rightfully ours. Some of the resulting crimes have also been quite bizarre.

In one truly extreme case, a man built a hotel in the late 19th century that was actually specially designed for murdering selected staff and guests once he had gained access to their money by various means. To this day nobody knows exactly how many people perished there as his victims disappeared into acid baths and furnaces, but it is estimated to be a number approaching 200. Crimes of passion are little different, as in the case of a sky diver whose parachute was disabled by a jealous rival in a three-way love affair, resulting in his rapid descent to instant death. The technology may change, but the motives are timeless. We could find many more examples of coveting and its consequences, but let's get back to the 10th commandment.

It's quite tempting to view the wording of the 10th commandment as culturally irrelevant in this day and age, or at best a bit quaint. You may not want to own your neighbour's shabby old house with its leaky roof and cracked foundations. Perhaps uncharitably, you may feel not the slightest attraction towards your neighbour's unglamorous spouse, and you are probably quite certain there is no sign of an ox or a donkey in his back garden, let alone any servants. This is, after all, the 21st century! In the absence of any livestock, it is also likely that you have no designs on his ancient beige station wagon either. In short, you might well think you don't want anything he owns.

Alas, that response would be to miss entirely the principle that God is laying down in this commandment. I said earlier that these Commandments are systemic, they aren't just a simple list of do's and don'ts. We cannot, in a reductionist way, look at each commandment in isolation and make real sense of God's moral law.

The 10th commandment illustrates this perfectly, because here God is telling us to be content, to be thankful for what He has given us. The 10th commandment provides a vital safeguard against breaking other preceding commandments, and it is intended to help us act responsibly towards our fellow human beings. All the evidence, both ancient and modern, shows the crucial need for this safeguard. Because, as we have already seen, from a covetous attitude, a disastrous array of sinful activity easily follows.

It is still tempting to think that none of this seriously applies to us, and to look at some of the awful examples of wickedness both old and new that have been driven by covetousness, and think we really aren't like that here in our quiet, comfortable, middle class suburb. OK, we might occasionally be a bit economical with the truth, we might sometimes have uncharitable thoughts about an irritating neighbour, or relatives, or parents. And in desperation we may have even "borrowed" a bit of loose change from the housekeeping jar on the fridge, but generally speaking, we've been pretty straight.

Sorry to say, this just doesn't cut it. In *Matt 5* Jesus blows that out of the water in the Sermon on the Mount. The idea there might be some sort of literal or legalistic comfort zone we could hope to construct for ourselves is a dangerous delusion. Jesus explains the real standard God expects from all of us, in both our attitude and our actions. He makes it clear that obeying the literal letter of the Law is not enough. This was the fatal preoccupation of the pharisees of His day. No, says Jesus, breaching God's Law by attitude alone is a direct failure of righteous behaviour.

He gives us two quite uncomfortable practical examples. In **Matt 5:21,22** He explains that hatred is the same as murder, and then in **Matt 5:27**, He goes on to warn us that misplaced sexual desire is no better than the physical act itself. Failure of attitude is dangerous, and it can lead to the discontent which causes coveting in one form or another. This is a very tough standard, which in one way or another, every last one of us inevitably fails.

So it is vital we understand that discontent and all that flows from it is one of the great dangers to us on our spiritual journey as Christians. Happily, Paul offers us really encouraging advice about the benefits of being content in *1Tim 6:6-10*.

> *Now there is great gain in godliness with contentment,*
> *for we brought nothing into the world, and we*
> *cannot take anything out of the world.*

We need to remember that when we get to heaven, God isn't going to make the size of our bank balance, which university (if any) we attended, or what job we had, a condition of entry. The poorest and humblest believer from a third world village and the multi-millionaire merchant banker will both stand before the Lord with exactly the same status. The Lord's concern will be that we know and believe Jesus died and rose to take the penalty for our sins and having believed, live in Christ.

Living in an affluent first world country constantly pushes us to want more and more, and modern marketing often uses the strategy of discontent to try and drive us down this path. So we must ask, is all ambition inherently wrong? Are Christians expected to be grey and gloomy losers? Should we feel guilty about success, or about living in comfortable circumstances?

The answer is no! What is wrong is a preoccupation with ourselves, with wanting to acquire more things than we really need, and in being unwilling to share what God has given us with others who are in genuine need. If God is replaced by a preoccupation with self and self gratification, that is the fatal error. This can turn our otherwise well motivated aspirations into idolatry, fuelling discontent that all too easily results in sinful behaviour. Jesus specifically warns us against the sort of discontent I've been talking about, and in **Matt 6:25-33** He challenges us to trust in God's provision for us.

Therefore I tell you, do not be anxious about your life, what you will eat or what you will drink, nor about your body, what you will put on. Is not life more important than food, and the body more than clothing? Look at the birds of the air: they neither sow nor reap nor gather into barns, and yet your heavenly Father feeds them. Are you not of more value than they? And which of you by being anxious can add a single hour to his span of life? And why are you anxious about clothing? Consider the lilies of the field, how they grow: they neither toil nor spin, yet I tell you, even Solomon in all his glory was not arrayed like one of these.

But if God so clothes the grass of the field, which today
is alive and tomorrow is thrown into the oven, will he
not much more clothe you, O you of little faith?
Therefore do not be anxious, saying, 'What shall we eat?'
or 'What shall we drink?' or 'What shall we wear?'
For the Gentiles seek after all these things, and your
heavenly Father knows that you need them all.
But seek first his kingdom and his righteousness,
and all these things will be added to you.

We need to claim that last promise every day. I am constantly challenged to remember that every day and every hour not only am I on God's time, but I am also always in His care. Our challenge is to keep the Lord who made us and saved us front and centre every day in everything that we do.

It sounds easy enough, but it is often really hard, isn't it? Our society constantly encourages us to believe that the acquisition of this or that will bring us greater happiness. All too easily we are seduced into thinking, if only I had the money for this, if only I was as successful as my friends, if only I had a better job, if only I could meet the right guy or girl (there's a whole message on trusting God in that one!), if only things in my church were organised differently,... the "if only" list is endless. Then, we tell ourselves, I'd be more content, then my Christian life and witness would be so much better. But deep down we need to recognise that this is just one of Satan's lies and snares.

Happily, in the providence of God the temptation to discontent and coveting does not have to end in disasters like the life of Bernie Madoff or the infidelity of David and Bathsheba. I love the case of Asaph. This man is a quiet Old Testament hero. Asaph was the temple music director in David's reign, and sadly lived long enough to see the golden age of Israel disintegrate under Solomon. He saw his own family members killed, and he saw greed and corruption take over in Israel. It just became everyone for themselves. Psalm 73 is the painfully honest account of this godly man's struggle with covetousness in truly awful times. Asaph was a small time operator compared to his well-off neighbours, and his personal situation really bugged him. I have this mental picture of a modern day Asaph; a talented musician whose day job isn't well paid and who never has much spare cash. Off he goes each week to choir practice in his beat up old car, but he can't help eyeing off the gleaming new sportscar in his neighbour's driveway. He takes his annual vacation in a small coastal caravan park well aware that his sun-tanned neighbours go off on expensive Pacific cruises. How he envies these guys! They seem so successful, so healthy, and so stress free. What has godly behaviour done for me, he asks himself? It is a timeless story as ***Psalm 73 vs3&4*** recounts:

For I was envious of the arrogant when I
saw the prosperity of the wicked.
For they have no pangs until death;
their bodies are fat and sleek.
They are not in trouble as others are; they are
not stricken like the rest of mankind.
Vs13&14:
All in vain have I kept my heart clean and
washed my hands in innocence.
For all the day long I have been stricken
and rebuked every morning.

This is a classic case of envy and would-be covetousness that we can all relate to. Asaph is consumed by the apparent failure of his faith to produce any immediate rewards, and so his trust in God falters. Fortunately his story has a happy ending. Despite the social and material pressures around him, he doesn't lose the spiritual plot, and by God's grace comes to recognise that these rich and arrogant people are only temporary winners, and that they will all ultimately face God's judgement. His humble confession in *Psalm 73:21-24* must surely strike a chord with all of us:

> *When my soul was embittered, when*
> *I was pricked in heart,*
> *I was brutish and ignorant; I was like a beast toward you.*
> *Nevertheless, I am continually with*
> *you; you hold my right hand.*
> *You guide me with your counsel, and*
> *afterward you will receive me to glory.*

Asaph finally recognised what was happening to him: he sees the dangers of abandoning his trust in God and giving way to envying, of falling into the trap of coveting the "now" when he already has something money can never buy. He realises that he has the greatest gift of all, God's eternal care and salvation. Nearly three millennia later we should thank the Lord every day that He continues to offer us this same gift without price. Like Asaph, we should thank the Lord for His provision of love and salvation every single day.

The 10th commandment has an unequivocal message for us from God. Trust me, He says! God may want us rich, he may want us poor, he may want us in work that we like or dislike, he may want us married, he may want us single. Not all of these outcomes will be judged by the world as the best and most successful options for us. Nor are all of these the easiest options for us to accept. But above all else, God wants us to trust Him, and trust that He always has our very best interests at heart. And why wouldn't we? If we really believe that Jesus died and rose for us, if we really believe that we are saved for all eternity by God's grace alone, then is it such a big ask to trust God's care and provision in the day to day life He has planned for each of us here?

One thing is absolutely certain. Whatever its ups and downs, our life can never be the rich and fulfilling experience God intends for us without that trust. So, the last of the commandments is an important key to all God's Ten Commandments as our blueprint for living. The Bible assures us that the Law of the Lord is perfect, and this is true in both a moral and a systemic sense. Morally because it covers every aspect of human conduct, and systemically because the commandments are self consistent and interdependent as a system. We live redeemed by the grace of God in Christ, but we should never forget that our lives and our righteousness are still measured by the perfect standard of God's Law as Jesus has explained it.

As a quick summary, let me finish by returning to the two issues I raised at the beginning.

Firstly, covetousness driven by envy or discontent is deadly dangerous because it encourages us to break God's law in so many ways, and in turn can breed a failure to trust God in everything.

Secondly, the 10th commandment illustrates the perfection of God's wisdom in the Law as a design for living. It is a protection against breaking other commandments and it encourages us to have complete trust in God's provision and purposes for us, no matter what our personal situation.

Across 3000 years of time, I'll give the faithful Asaph the last word in *Psalm 73:28*:

But as for me, it is good to be near God. I have made the Lord God my refuge that I may tell of your works".

We should ask God to help us to be like Asaph in our daily walk, to trust Him and make Him our constant refuge in every situation and so in our lives to give witness every day to those around us of His redeeming grace at work within us.

Chapter 9
THE BIG BANG

D id the universe really start from a Big Bang? On current scientific evidence it would seem so. Until about sixty years ago, most scientists thought that the universe had always been much as it is now, but then early in the 20th century astronomers like Edwin Hubble and others, found that the data they were observing fitted better with an expanding universe model rather than one which was simply static. Even Einstein, who had originally favoured the idea of a static universe, concluded that an expanding universe was better aligned with his theories. Unsurprisingly then, during the first half of the 20th century theories about the origins of the universe and whether it was expanding, static or shrinking, were much debated in the scientific community. Some continued to support the long held steady state theory while there were others convinced that the universe had a finite starting point and has been expanding ever since in what has become popularly known as "The Big Bang" theory. Then in 1964 the first real observable evidence supporting the validity of this so-called "Big Bang" theory came to light quite by accident.

Two American radio astronomers at the famed Bell Telephone research labs, the place where the transistor was invented, were working on a large experimental horn shaped radio antenna that was originally designed to detect very weak radio signals reflected from satellites. They, however, wanted to use it to analyse signals from the Milky Way. But first, they had to identify and eliminate the other much stronger but irrelevant signals it also picked up from earthly sources. Things like signals from radar systems, broadcast transmitters and so on. Having eliminated all these known but unwanted signal sources, they found they still had a problem. They kept picking up a strange unidentifiable background noise which seemed to come from everywhere. First of all they thought the antenna was faulty, and at one point that maybe the noise was the result of bird droppings from pigeons nesting in the horn! So they literally cleaned out the horn and got rid of the birds, but the noise persisted. In the end it turned out that what they were receiving was actually background cosmic noise with characteristics which matched those predicted by the Big Bang theory. For this initially accidental discovery the two Bell Labs scientists concerned were later awarded the Nobel Prize for what turned out to be their very important, if rather unexpected, breakthrough. Later discoveries have continued to strengthen the evidence for an expanding universe making it now the most generally accepted theory explaining its origins.

According to the Big Bang theory, the universe originated from a cosmic explosion at a single point. If the universe has a discrete point of origin, it also follows that time and space as we know it only came into existence when the universe itself was created. As a Christian, this makes perfect sense to me. The Lord of all Creation surely must operate outside the constraints of time and space as we know them, and which He Himself had brought into existence in the first place. So it is no wonder that our human attempts to understand the immense scale of His wonderful creation just send our heads spinning!

For all of recorded history, mankind has marvelled at the stars and our place in the observable universe, even to the point of superstition and fortune telling. Yet in reality, the stars we see in the night sky are evidence of something far greater, and far beyond the limited speculations of mankind. They are the evidence of God's astonishing creation writ large. Modern telescopes, particularly those like the Hubble and the James Webb, which orbit the planet outside the distortions of earth's atmosphere, have progressively revealed a universe that is more immense, more complex and more breathtakingly beautiful than anything we could have ever imagined.

Billions upon billions of stars, countless galaxies, and huge gas clouds extend as far as our equipment can see. And that's only the 5% which is visible to us. The other 95%, we only know as "dark matter" and "dark energy", is invisible and we only know it's there because of its gravitational effects on stars.

We've always wondered where all this fabulous cosmic complexity came from. Until evidence validating the Big Bang theory emerged, as I mentioned earlier, it was more generally assumed that the universe was in a steady state, and had always just been there. That suited atheists just fine, because it needed no creator, no deity, nothing and nobody to get things started. Then came the Big Bang theory, which put atheists in the uncomfortable position of having to explain the really hard question. How did it all begin?

Alas, it gets worse for atheists. Astrophysics has also shown that the properties of the Big Bang must have been unbelievably precise, or our universe would never have existed. Distinguished astrophysicist the late Stephen Hawking, who was not a Christian, observed:

> "If the rate of expansion one second after the big bang had been smaller by even one part in a hundred thousand million million, the universe would have re-collapsed before it reached its present size ..."The odds against a universe like ours emerging from the Big Bang, are enormous."

Distinguished astronomer and publicly vocal atheist Sir Fred Hoyle who hated the idea of a big bang (even though he was the one who actually invented the term), eventually grudgingly said:

> "A commonsense interpretation of the facts suggests that a super-intellect has monkeyed with the physics as well as with chemistry and biology, and that there are no blind forces worth speaking about in nature".

The eminent theoretical physicist Paul Davies (also not a Christian) admitted:

> "Through my scientific work I have come to believe more and more strongly that the universe is put together with an ingenuity so astonishing that I cannot accept it as brute fact...I cannot believe that our existence in this universe is a mere quirk of fate...we are truly meant to be here".

What confronts these guys is overwhelming evidence that not only did it require extremely precise conditions for our universe to exist at all, but that it is also extremely orderly. There is nothing random or chaotic about it. Instead it operates under elegant laws that have allowed mathematicians to make many theoretical predictions about its physical properties even before their actual discovery. This surely cannot be an accident.

Let me offer a couple of examples. As I explained in Chapter 4, in the 1860s mathematician and devout Christian James Clerk Maxwell devised four equations that are of fundamental importance to the theoretical foundations of modern electrical engineering. Amongst other things, his work predicted the possibility of radio communication. Then some 20 years later, and inspired by Maxwell's mathematics, the German physicist Heinrich Hertz built equipment that demonstrated radio was a practical possibility; his experiments proved that Maxwell's predictions were right. These same equations remain today as the mathematical foundation of all modern electronics.

Around 900 years ago the Italian scholar Leonardo Fibonacci devised a mathematical number series that describes many of the patterns seen every day in nature on things like pineapples, pine cones, plant leaves, sunflowers, sea shells and much more. Fibbonacci's series demonstrates something of the incredible mathematical order throughout the natural world. We do not live in the outcome of some chaotic, random, cosmic accident.

If the odds of the universe coming into existence at all were tiny, the odds of there being the right conditions for life within it are even smaller again. We have long wondered if there is other life out there in the vast reaches of space, but so far, despite the intense efforts of many researchers, no one has found any real evidence at all. Fifty years ago astronomers were quite optimistic about finding extra-terrestrial life, but now realise that the odds of another planet in another solar system supporting life are actually incredibly tiny. Scientists today acknowledge that it is amazing even planet earth supports life! But it only does so because a number of factors are just right. This is called the "Goldilocks Principle" referring of course to the well known fairy tale of "The Three Bears". Factors which contribute to earth sustaining life include: our distance from the sun, earth's size, its mass, its magnetic field, the moon being perfectly placed to control tides, our 23.5 degree axial tilt and 24 hour rotation, the thickness of the earth's crust, and our plentiful supply of water. Our planetary conditions are all just right for supporting life. Could this too, really just be an accident?

I don't think so. Paul reminds us of this and God's controlling hand in creation in **Colossians 1:16&17:**

For by him all things were created, in heaven and on earth, visible and invisible, whether thrones or dominions or rulers or authorities – all things were created through him and for him. And he is before all things, and in him all things hold together.

Yet despite all the evidence of a creator devising and maintaining the amazing order and precision in our universe, noted atheists like Richard Dawkins still reject it all:

> "The universe that we observe has precisely the properties we should expect if there is, at bottom, no design, no purpose, no evil, no good, nothing but pitiless indifference."

Paul warns us in **Romans 1:18-23** that we should expect just this sort of perverse reaction to the evidence of God's hand in the creation around us as an outcome of our misplaced arrogance.

For the wrath of God is revealed from heaven against
all ungodliness and unrighteousness of men, who
by their unrighteousness suppress the truth.

For what can be known about God is plain to them, because
God has shown it to them. For his invisible attributes,
namely, his eternal power and divine nature, have been
clearly perceived, ever since the creation of the world, in the
things that have been made. So they are without excuse.

For although they knew God, they did not honour him
as God or give thanks to him, but they became futile in
their thinking, and their foolish hearts were darkened.
Claiming to be wise, they became fools, and exchanged
the glory of the immortal God for images resembling
mortal man and birds and animals and creeping things.

I could go on assembling physical evidence which makes any claim that our existence here has happened purely by chance seem close to complete nonsense. But this is not a physics lecture, and very importantly, not an attempt to prove the existence of God using argument by design, because I know it would certainly still fail, as it always has, to convince many unbelievers.

Let me come instead to **Psalm 19**, which I think gives us a key to the connection between science and faith. It tells us in eloquent poetic language that the universe constantly speaks to us of God the Creator, of the One working far beyond the dimensions of space and time as we know them, and on a scale we can barely begin to comprehend. But it also tells us that in the end, it is only a personal walk of faith in the light of God's Word which can make our relationship with Him possible. It is this and this alone, which will allow us to make any sense of the amazing creation in which we live.

Here we are, a speck of dust in the universe on a small planet amongst billions of stars. How can we actually matter at all? Well, we know we do, because, by an incomprehensible miracle of grace, God entered His own creation, and appeared amongst us in human form to reconcile us to Himself. What could be more amazing than that?

Before we go any further, a word about the Psalms. Much of the Bible provides us with a progressive, historic and prophetic revelation of the Kingdom of God. But the Psalms are different because of the very personal way they record a 3000 year old response of believers to the revelation of God's purposes for them, and their response is just as valid for us today as it was then. Psalm literally means "song for musical accompaniment". The great 19thC preacher Charles Spurgeon said the Psalms were *"a complete armory for life's battles, and perfect supply for Life's needs"*, and we might add, very happily have been an ongoing inspiration for generations of gospel song writers!

One of the remarkable things about the Psalms, and the revelation of God they provide, is that this revelation comes through the eyes of people still awaiting the coming of their Messiah. It comes through the eyes of people who had only seen a partial unfolding of salvation history. So if God's people of that time could respond so powerfully and so poetically to His greatness as the Lord of all creation, to His personal presence, and to His redeeming grace, how much more should this be true for us. We who know with certainty that Jesus is the fulfillment of God's revelation of Himself and His Kingdom!

Psalm 19 has two distinct parts; verses 1-6, and verses 7-14, and they are so different that some commentators have argued it is really two separate psalms. Personally, I seriously doubt this. I think there is a message of fundamental importance about the nature of God's relationship with us that is purposely revealed by the great contrast between the two parts of this psalm.

> *The heavens declare the glory of God, and the sky*
> *above proclaims his handiwork. Day to day pours out*
> *speech, and night to night reveals knowledge.*

These introductory and well known verses are an affirmation of the presence of God through the evidence of the all-pervasive splendour of His creation, and describe the way this same creation speaks to everyone everywhere of its Creator. Look around you says the Psalmist, in verses 1 & 2, the heavens remind us, by day and by night, of the permanent, visible, and inescapable hand of God seen in the utter magnificence of His creation. It is all there, shouting at you!

Verses 3 & 4 reinforce this theme:

> *There is no speech, nor are there words,*
> *whose voice is not heard.*
> *Their voice goes out through all the earth, and their words to*
> *the end of the world. In them he has set a tent for the sun,*

The metaphorical language used here reminds us that the testimony of creation is so powerful it is just as if it were literally speaking and shouting to every living creature in every known language about the works of God.

The sun becomes the focus of poetic attention at the end of verse 4 and on into verses 5 & 6. So why this extraordinary vision of the sun emerging like a bridegroom or an athlete? Today, we take the sun pretty much for granted, but in the ancient world it dominated life, and was certainly never taken for granted. Most activities required daylight - artificial light was weak and primitive. Until quite recent times, prior to the invention of first gas and then electric lighting, people feared the darkness of the night when evil and chaos could flourish. The health and prosperity of the agricultural economies in the ancient world depended absolutely on the power of the sun, so unsurprisingly it is depicted here as the most spectacular and obvious manifestation of God's hand at work. Its unfailing power, the absolute predictability of its daily passage, and the all-pervasive nature of its light and heat reflect the qualities of God Himself.

This reference also puts the sun in its proper place. Sun worship was very common in the religious life of the ancient world. The Babylonians and the Egyptians worshipped sun gods, and even wrote hymns to them. But here, the sun in all its magnificence is not seen as a God but rather as a very powerful voice in nature that speaks of God as the Creator. It is a specific recognition of God's provision rather than treating the sun as one of the smorgasbord of occasional deities to be appeased by superstitious and ignorant people. And very importantly, it reflects a monotheistic world view which set the people of Israel apart from other ancient civilisations.

Then in verse 7 the focus of this Psalm seems to shift gear dramatically; or does it? Suddenly, the focus is no longer on the observable Creation, but turns instead to the Law of God as the key to knowing God personally. What does the Law of God mean here? It means all of God's revelation of Himself through His Word. In contrast to describing the wonder of Creation, verses 7 to 11 shift the focus to tell us of God's personal revelation of Himself in a far more intimate and far more challenging way to each one of us. A personal revelation that is entirely and absolutely essential to our salvation.

This starts in verse 7 by describing the qualities of God's Law:

The Law of the Lord is perfect - just like Creation before the fall.

Reviving the soul - it is the means to salvation, in it we find God's redeeming grace, and our means to becoming and remaining spiritually alive.

The statutes of the LORD are trustworthy - God's Word offers truth and certainty, it can withstand all human attack. Nothing over thousands of years from the brutality of the Assyrians, to the Dark Ages, to the worst excesses of modern totalitarianism, atheism, or modern terrorism, has in any way dimmed its power. Jesus promised in Matt **24:35** that:

> *"heaven and earth may pass away but*
> *my words will not pass away."*

making wise the simple - the power of salvation, and all the essential wisdom and insight for daily life, are available to anyone through God's Word. It is not about formal education or intelligence.

The Psalmist continues in verse 8:

The precepts of the LORD are right - this reminds us of the perfection of God's directions to us in His Word.

rejoicing the heart - this begins a theme taken up again in verse 10 that speaks of the sense of inner joy and peace which only comes when we are obedient believers in the Word of God. Something that simply cannot be bought with money.

The commandment of the LORD is pure - reminding us again of the inherent perfection of God's Word.

enlightening the eyes - when we view the world through the Word of God, we see everything, the society we live in and our own actions, in the light of God's standards. We can never hope to comprehend and evaluate the world around us, or understand its complexity, on our own. It is only in the light of God's Word that we have any means of understanding what actually matters.

These two great verses summarise in one sweep the qualities of God's Word, and the powerful effect it can have. Many stories illustrate the truth of verses 8&9. Some time ago, one of the weekend papers included the story of a woman going out with a guy, and although she liked him, had some real reservations because he said he was a Christian. So she started reading the Bible, beginning with the Gospels. She wanted to be able to debate this potential stumbling block with him. God spoke to her through His Word; the reality of who Jesus really is hit her like a bombshell, and she accepted Him as her Lord and Saviour. No preaching, just the power of God's Word, God's Law at work! So it comes as no surprise that the Gideons, a worldwide organisation that provides Bibles in all sorts of places, have many stories to tell of people who have come to a real and active Christian faith simply from reading bibles they have found in places like hotel bedrooms.

Verse 9 goes on to explain that the outcome of accepting God's Word must be a recognition of the eternal, complete holiness of God and of His judgements.

> *the fear of the LORD is clean, enduring forever; the rules*
> *of the LORD are true, and righteous altogether.*

Don't be put off by the word "fear". Modern cultural arrogance means that humility in any form isn't much admired. The word is used here to describe our recognition of the awesome, holy, loving and omnipotent creator God whom we serve, the one who formed the amazing universe in which we live. That is true fear of the Lord, not mindless cringing obeisance to some uncaring all-powerful entity ready to zap us into a pile of grey ash for making the slightest mistake.

Verse 10 goes on to answer the question: how then do you put a value on the Word and the judgements of God?

> *More to be desired are they than gold, even much fine gold;*
> *sweeter also than honey and drippings of the honeycomb.*

Gold has always been the most valuable amongst precious metals, and for much of history it has symbolised the pinnacle of wealth. Honey gets mentioned 58 times in the Bible, mostly symbolising the best of food (as in the land flowing with milk and honey). So verse 10 is basically saying that God's Word is more precious, more valuable than anything material that wealth or good living can provide.

Why then is God's Word of such value?

> *Moreover, by them is your servant warned;*
> *in keeping them there is great reward.*

Understanding and obeying the Word of God is what stands between us and eternity. Only by His Word are we able to recognise the perfection, the holiness, and the majesty of God, and only by the light it gives our eyes (as verse 8 explained) can we see just how imperfect and how sinful we really are. Only by His Word do we know that Jesus died and rose to redeem us and offer that redemption to all mankind.

This drives the psalmist to his knees in verse 12 & 13, praying to God a prayer that we should all pray.

> *Who can discern his errors? Declare me*
> *innocent from hidden faults.*
> *Keep back your servant also from presumptuous sins;*
> *let them not have dominion over me! Then I shall be*
> *blameless, and innocent of great transgression.*

Firstly, we are asked to acknowledge that we don't understand the extent of our own sinfulness, asking forgiveness for all the known and unknown ways in which we fail to meet the standards of our perfect and holy God. Secondly we need to ask protection from "willful sins"; acts of rebellion against God done knowing that they are wrong, knowing they fail God's expectations and standards for our social, moral and intellectual behaviour. No Christian is immune from this sort of temptation, and nothing is more potentially damaging to our spiritual lives.

So the psalmist comes to one inescapable conclusion; impressive as it is, it is not the scale, beauty and grandeur of God's creation that brings him to his knees, casting himself on the mercy and grace of God. No, it's the intensely personal and piercing light of God's Word which lets him see himself as he really is. And 3000 years on, it is absolutely no different for you and for me.

The psalmist ends in verse 14 by praying:

Let the words of my mouth and the meditation of my heart be acceptable in your sight, O Lord , my Rock and my Redeemer.

This is a prayer for every believer and every inquirer; that God will make all our thoughts and actions pleasing to Him, He who is our Rock, our immovable Creator, and best of all, our Redeemer. Is there any one of us who can be confident that all our thoughts and actions are already entirely pleasing to God? I don't think so.

This psalm is remarkable because it spans the totality of God's creation and at the same time, makes crystal clear His purposes for us as individuals. It acknowledges the glory of physical creation that shouts through the heavens of the works of God, yet warns that even in seeing His hand at work we may choose to reject Him. Then in the dramatic switch at verse 7 we see that only God's own Word can reveal Him to us personally when we accept Jesus as our Lord and Saviour. Only this allows us to truly understand what it means to live in God's creation. Theories like the "big bang", intriguing as they may be in helping us understand the origins of Creation, can never connect us eternally with our Creator God. Only the unique individual experience of accepting Jesus can give us the promise of a personal and eternal relationship with God, the promise of a relationship with Him that will continue forever outside present time and space as we know it, when Jesus returns.

Chapter 10

THE SECOND COMING

A headline in the New York times of June 26th, 1922 ran as follows:

Second Coming Fixed for 1925 or by 1949

The article quotes one A.H. MacMillan, General Manager of the International Bible Students Association, who claimed that all the portents were there and citing a recent description of world affairs given by then British Prime Minister Lloyd George as evidence that all the signs of Christ's imminent return were at hand. MacMillan even went on to claim that once Christ returns we will all start growing young again, but apparently didn't indicate where the process stops, which could prove to be a bit of a worry. He also suggested that we will reverse all our misdeeds, and right all our past wrongs. I can only say that such a scheme would make this particular sinner one very busy boy!

Speculation about the return of Jesus, made in this case just over 100 years ago and claiming to know the time and place when Our Lord will return (otherwise known as The Second Coming), has been around ever since the resurrection. A brief internet search led me at one point to a website rather appropriately called www.armageddon-online.org which offered a very long list of failed predictions of the second coming scattered through almost every century since the time of Christ Himself. 500AD seemed very likely to some, and 1000 AD was a near certainty for others, but when nothing happened, its proponents said they'd forgotten to factor in the length of Jesus's life, and so 1033AD was really it. Martin Luther briefly speculated on 1530 before coming to his senses, and 1697 was popular with several Anglican clerics. Even Jonathon Edwards, a key figure in the 18th century evangelical revival and a former president of Princeton University, predicted it would all happen in 1866 when the papacy ended.

In a book called "Dispensational Truth", published in 1918, and doubtless influenced by the horrors of World War I, the author Clarence Larkin claimed that "at no time in the history of the Christian Church have the conditions necessary to the Lord's return been so completely fulfilled" and predicted AD 2000 as "the date". In 1972 Don Stanton published a book arguing that all the signs indicated that the end of the age was near. He even quoted a former Chancellor of the University of Chicago as saying "I cannot foresee any future to our known world after nine years". Another unnamed scientist declared "genetic engineering may be modern man's only hope to preserve a small part of his society when civilization self-destructs some time in the next thirty years".

Let me end this brief parade of eschatological speculations with the more recent writings of Ronald Weinland, who claimed on his website (www.the-end.com) that he was one of God's two special witnesses mentioned in Revelation 11, and predicted that 2008 would usher in the last days and three and a half years of tribulation (including the demise of the USA). And there are many more examples like these to be found in print and on the internet.

Two common factors seem to influence people preoccupied with predicting Christ's return. The first is an absolute conviction that the local times and events in which they live are the first ever which meet all the conditions for the end time and the return of Jesus. The second is a focus on the book of **Revelation**; and it is here that many of the more imaginative ideas about Christ's return originate. Many misunderstandings begin when people treat this book as literal future doomsday prophesy, which it is not. The book of **Revelation** is primarily about the final victory already won against sin and death for all of human history in the person and the work of Our Lord Jesus Christ. Like all scripture, it was written for Christians in every age, but it was also especially intended to encourage Christians in the churches of Asia Minor during times of terrible persecution within the Roman Empire. It is a book that is first and last about the Gospel, and about the consequences for all creation that follow from the life, death and resurrection of Our Lord as the pivot point of all human history. In fact, the whole Bible, not just **Revelation**, looks forward to both the first and second coming of Jesus as the fulfillment of God's covenantal promise of salvation to all mankind.

Some misunderstandings also arise because Revelation was written in an apocalyptic and coded literary style using imagery generally unfamiliar to modern readers. For this reason it can be very misleading if read literally and without putting its contents into the wider context of the rest of Scripture.

So it is not surprising that it has been the inspiration for some rather imaginative but not necessarily biblically factual material which has appeared over the years in the public domain, as I think my preceding examples amply demonstrate.

If understanding this book is a problem to you, I strongly recommend two works written by internationally respected Christian scholars which explain Revelation as a book about the Gospel and the Kingdom of God rather than as a rather lurid prophesy about ultimate catastrophe. These are Graeme Goldsworthy's **"The Lamb and The Lion"**, and Paul Barnett's **"Apocalypse Now and Then"**.

The key point I want to make from my brief survey of these sometimes fanciful predictions is that speculation about when Jesus will return is a counterproductive distraction when the Bible plainly and explicitly tells us we <u>cannot</u> know this. Yet it seems from what Jesus taught His disciples as recorded in *Mathew 24,* that even they were not exempt from a curiosity that has been common to Christians through the ages.

Nothing could be clearer than the answer Jesus gave to His disciples in *Matthew 25:36* when they asked about His return:

> *"No one knows about that day or hour, not even the angels in heaven, nor the Son, but only the Father."*

Now if Jesus Himself can say "even I don't know", why then across the past 2000 years have some Christians believed they know better? What matters is that we understand what Jesus Himself taught His disciples about His return, and we should beware of being seduced by the small group of rather vocal writers and would-be prophets over the centuries who, for whatever motives, have deluded themselves into believing that they know more about the future than the Lord Himself has been prepared to reveal to us in His Word.

When we look at **Matthew 24 & 25** it becomes clear that what matters is not <u>when</u> but <u>why</u> Jesus is going to return and <u>what</u> we should be doing now. This is what the Bible is focussed on and is what it talks about. On the other hand, it is deliberately silent on <u>when</u> Jesus will return. This approach will help us understand what the Bible teaches about the Second Coming rather than trying to second-guess God's unrevealed timetable for His plans.

In the first half of **Matthew 24** we find Jesus predicting the destruction of the Jerusalem temple. Given its absolutely pre-eminent place in Jewish religious life, this must have been a pretty disquieting piece of prophesy for the disciples to absorb. So it is no surprise that we learn in **Matthew 24:3** they took Jesus aside to question Him more closely about this.

As he sat on the Mount of Olives, the disciples came to him privately, saying, "Tell us, when will these things be, and what will be the sign of your coming and of the close of the age?"

What Jesus has to say in reply to their question, not apocalyptic speculation, provides the best possible basis for our understanding of His return.

In the first half of **Matthew 24** Jesus specifically warns His disciples, and us, against jumping to conclusions about the future. He warns there will be false prophets claiming to be Him. He warns of times of great tribulation, and terrible suffering. But was this really about events which were actual precursors to the end of the world? Apparently not. Wars, natural disasters, persecution and suffering, always have and always will be part of sinful human history. They remain inherent to our fallen world until Jesus returns. But Jesus says that they are not necessarily a sign of the end of the age.

Matthew 24:15-28 seems most likely to refer to the coming destruction of Jerusalem by the Romans as they brutally crushed one of several Jewish rebellions. It is unlikely to refer to a final apocalypse, and events in history bear this out. In AD 66 a Jewish rebellion commenced against Roman occupation in which the temple was destroyed, and culminated in a siege in which the Romans tried to starve out the rebel Jews who made their last stand in the fortifications of Masada which they had captured previously from the Romans. The physical evidence of the Roman ramp built to breach Masada remains to this day. There was unimaginable hardship and suffering, including cannibalism, and even false messiahs emerged. In AD 70 the Romans stormed the city, and reduced almost everything to rubble, including the temple. A million Jews died, and about 100,000 were taken captive. This resulted in a complete collapse of their social order, and this is the subject of Christ's warning about imminent cataclysmic events, including the perils of escape into the Judean hills in harsh winter weather, the terrible plight of pregnant women, and the hazards of limits to travel on the sabbath.

The Roman empire itself became rather unstable after Nero died in AD68 and various would-be Caesars laid claim to power. Writers of the period, quite unconcerned with Jerusalem and its fate, thought the whole world was about to end. This period of enormous upheaval is described in richly figurative language, especially in verse 29, but it is not about the end of the world, even though the suffering and upheavals must have seemed like it at the time. At best, it was a small reflection of events yet to come in the very last days.

Then in *Matthew 24:26&27*, Jesus reminds His disciples that when He comes again, it won't be associated with localised events like a Jewish rebellion. When He returns the whole world will see Him instantly, everyone will know without any doubt that He is the Lord of all and that His return consummates His victory already won at Calvary as he rules over a new heaven and a new earth of perfect holiness. This is the <u>why</u> of His return.

Let me pause here to remind readers that the major function of prophesy is often not to pinpoint exactly <u>when</u> future specific events such as Christ's coming will occur. Its purpose is to provide us with certainty about God's plans for His creation and us as individuals, and to give a sombre warning to unbelievers. The Jews of Jesus's time are a classic example of failure to understand this. They were desperate to know <u>when</u> their messiah would come; they wanted an immediate political solution to their problems as an occupied country. So the temple had shifted in their hearts and minds from being a symbol of the covenantal promise of salvation that undergirds all salvation history and permeates the whole Bible, simply to being a symbol of Jewish political identity. Result? They failed absolutely to recognise Jesus and had no understanding of the personal salvation that He brought in fulfillment of God's promises to them through His prophets in the Old Testament.

We should learn from this. We should keep our hearts fixed on understanding, and on participating in the miracle of grace we enjoy through God's revelation of His Kingdom in the coming of Christ. This is what we really celebrate at Christmas. This again is the <u>why</u> of the coming of Christ. This is what the Bible concentrates on, not on providing detailed roadmaps of the future. ***Matthew 24:30-35*** are debated by scholars, but many agree that their language and context make most sense as the completion of Jesus's answer to the Disciples' question about events after the destruction of the temple rather than referring to the second coming.

The argument runs as follows. We know Jesus came to fulfill God's promise of salvation by paying the penalty for our sin and disobedience through His death and resurrection. In His first coming, we know by His resurrection He won the victory over sin and death once and for all time, and that His Second Coming will bring once and for all time the completion of God's promise and purpose for creation itself to its final fulfillment. *"Behold I make all things new"* He says in **Revelation 21**; and in consequence the effects of sin and death will be banished forever as God finally restores His creation to its original perfection. In that light, **Matthew 24:30-35** seem best understood as foreshadowing the growth of the church and the spread of the Gospel after Christ's ascension, a time in human history that as we now know has been one in which the gospel has prevailed and spread globally long after the might of Rome had collapsed and become nothing more than a chapter in the wider span of human history.

Then we come to **Matthew 24:36**, which is where I started out. Here, Jesus turns His attention again to the Disciples second question as they ask Him what signs will tell us about the end of the age and <u>when</u> you will return? And as we have already seen Jesus simply tells them;

> *But concerning that day and hour no one knows, not even the angels of heaven, nor the Son, but the Father only.*

This is an unequivocal statement that the return of Jesus will be at a time known and set by God the Father alone. And significantly, Paul and other New Testament writers echo just what Jesus says here; they don't try to pinpoint <u>when</u> Jesus will come. Instead, they consistently record their certainty that He will return; and they look forward to it eagerly.

Not only does Jesus tell us that we <u>cannot know</u> when He will return, but in **Matthew 24:37-41** He warns us that many people will get a terrible surprise. Life will seem to be going on absolutely normally, just as in Noah's time before the flood. People will be in cafes sipping their lattes, shopping, doing business, going on holidays, playing golf, you name it. There will be courting, weddings, parties, all the normal social round. And then, just when we least expect it, Jesus <u>will</u> return. I'm not too certain what the doomsday brigade, some of whom have made an industry out of reading Christ's imminent return into current historical events, actually make of this. Their version of events would have us believe that the times will be so ominous, and so awful, that it will be obvious to all those in the know that Jesus is about to reappear. But Jesus tells us just the opposite; that when He returns it will be at a time when things are going to seem fairly normal.

However, we need to take great heed of the point Jesus goes on to make in these verses. Not only will He return when we least expect it, but the truly awful tragedy is that so many people will be totally and completely unprepared for Him. In **Matthew 24:39-41** Jesus tells us:

> *so will be the coming of the Son of Man. Then two*
> *men will be in the field; one will be taken and one left.*
> *Two women will be grinding at the mill; one will be*
> *taken and one left. Therefore, stay awake, for you*
> *do not know on what day your Lord is coming.*

Here we have a picture of men and women working together, each pair sharing similar life styles, and apparently similar values. It could just as well be two accountants, two nurses, two shop assistants, two teachers, and I fear in some cases even two ministers.

In each case one will be ready for Jesus and the other will not. Commonality of purpose, of friendship, of appearance or even membership of the one church, will count for nothing here. And why? Because only one of each pair will have embraced God's saving grace in Christ, and so only that person of each pair will experience Jesus's promise and join Him when He returns. So I am duty bound to ask you, and to ask myself, will we be ready? The alternative does not bear thinking about.

What follows now is crucial to our understanding of the Second Coming. Be ready, says Jesus in *Matthew 24:42–44.*

> *Therefore, stay awake, for you do not know on what day your Lord is coming. But know this, that if the master of the house had known in what part of the night the thief was coming, he would have stayed awake and would not have let his house be broken into. Therefore you also must be ready, for the Son of Man is coming at an hour you do not expect.*

These words alone should impel us to be constant, faithful servants of the Gospel and certainly not to waste time on second guessing when the second coming will occur. It is of course only the first of five parables encouraging us to be prepared for Jesus's return. The story of the thief in the night is followed in *Matthew 24:45–51* by the sobering story of the unfaithful servant who abuses his position and is punished when his master returns as *Matthew 24:50&51* record.

> *The master of that servant will come on a day when he does not expect him and at an hour he does not know and will cut him in pieces and put him with the hypocrites. In that place there will be weeping and gnashing of teeth.*

This parable should also be a sobering reminder to us of the tragic failure in parts of the church today to teach and to defend basic Biblical truth and morality, and of the terrible consequences of giving way to populist liberalism.

The warnings flow on into chapter 25 with the series of parables Jesus taught on readiness. The case of the unfaithful servant, the case of the wise and foolish virgins, the story of the talents, and the separation of the sheep and the goats. All these parables have one common theme, namely that we have a personal responsibility to be ready for Jesus' coming and the evidence for our readiness will be in the way we live and behave as God's faithful servants. You know something is important when the Bible gives it a lot of air time, and the command to be faithful and ready is certainly one of those.

Arguments and speculation abound about the details of the way events will unfold between the resurrection and the Second Coming; and I haven't even uttered the word "millennium"! It is only really mentioned in one chapter of Revelation which should tell us not to let it pre-occupy us. Rather than engaging in what can become rather fanciful speculation, we simply need to accept that trying to figure out the detail of the last days is clearly discouraged by Jesus. It is, as I have said previously, largely a distraction.

What I believe really matters is this. The Bible makes it clear that God has limited Satan's power in this post-resurrection era and given His church both the opportunity, and a clear directive in both good times and in bad, to preach the good news of God's saving grace in Christ. Very importantly He has also given us the time and the means to bear witness to His deep love for His creation in Christ by our love and care for those in need of His grace and mercy, and not least in our nurture and care of our fellow believers. This is how we should spend the time before He returns.

We should also always remember that ever since the resurrection Christians have in fact been living in what the Bible calls "the last days". This is a much broader span of history than just some short intensive apocalyptic event . And why? Because the events of Calvary as I explained earlier are the pivot point of all history. Jesus tells us not to waste the opportunities available in this present era, but to use our time well, and so always to be ready for His return.

This message of readiness is repeated at length in the Gospel records of *Mark 13 and Luke 17*, and again by Paul in *1Thessalonians 4:13 to 5:11*. He starts by reminding his readers in *Ch5:1&2*:

> *Now concerning the times and the seasons, brothers,*
> *you have no need to have anything written to you.*
> *For you yourselves are fully aware that the day of*
> *the Lord will come like a thief in the night.*

And he ends with a great pastoral exhortation in *vs 9-11*:

> *For God has not destined us for wrath, but to obtain*
> *salvation through our Lord Jesus Christ, who died for*
> *us so that whether we are awake or asleep we might*
> *live with him. Therefore encourage one another and*
> *build one another up, just as you are doing.*

If we are saved by faith, if we really believe Jesus will return, we must live out our faith by assuming that this day might come at any moment and certainly when we least expect it. That was the mindset of the New Testament church, as you can see in *Romans 13:11, 12, I*

Cor 7:29, Phil 4:5, and *James 5:8*, and this should be the mindset of every responsible Christian in today's church until our Lord returns. Speculation about the <u>when</u> and the <u>how</u> of the Second Coming does absolutely nothing to prepare us to be with Jesus when He actually comes.

Let me conclude by trying to summarise what seem to me to be three of the key things we need to understand about the second coming.

The first is that when Jesus came the first time in human form, He fulfilled God's promise to reveal His Kingdom through the Messiah. When He died and rose from the grave, He provided the final victory over Satan, sin and death once and for all time as *Hebrews 9:24-28* tell us. This is what we celebrate at Christmas. "Born that man no more may die!"

The second is to acknowledge that we live in an era of struggle between good and evil, a time of ups and downs. But praise God, because of Jesus's first coming, this is an era when by the power of the Holy Spirit we can preach the Gospel and we can be saved by grace through faith in Jesus as He tells us in *Matthew 24:14:*

> *And this gospel of the kingdom will be proclaimed*
> *throughout the whole world as a testimony to*
> *all nations, and then the end will come.*

It is also again a great reminder that we should use this time well, and that we must be constantly ready for Jesus to return.

The third is to acknowledge that when Jesus does return, every eye will see Him, and every believer from every age will be with Christ. This will be a single time in human history when the final victory over sin and Satan won by Jesus in His first coming will be absolutely plain to everyone. There will be final judgement, the new heaven and new earth will be established and we will be returned to the perfect creation God always intended.

One important afterthought. Always remember that what we really celebrate at Christmas time is that God, by coming in human form has given us tangible evidence in the person of Jesus of the certainty of the final and eternal triumph of the Kingdom of God and of His love and goodness in all creation. It is proof of God's promise of the elimination of evil, and that we who believe in Jesus as our Saviour will be with Him forever. Our future is in the utterly trustworthy hands of God Himself, and the birth of Jesus is living proof of that. What a reason to celebrate Christmas, and to affirm it as His faithful servants by always remaining ready in expectation of His coming at any time.

John writes in R*ev 22 :*

> *"He who testifies to these things says,*
> *"Surely , I am coming soon."*

We must surely respond with John saying:

> *"Amen. Come Lord Jesus".*